the
bride's
instruction
manual

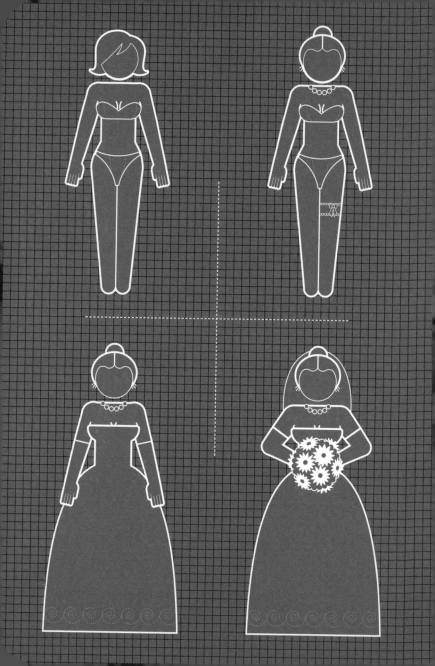

the bride's
instruction manual

HOW TO SURVIVE AND POSSIBLY EVEN ENJOY
THE BIGGEST DAY OF YOUR LIFE

by Carrie Denny

Illustrated by Paul Kepple and Scotty Reifsnyder

QUIRK BOOKS
PHILADELPHIA

Library of Congress Cataloging in Publication Number: 2008931238

ISBN: 978-1-59474-265-1

Printed in China

Typeset in Swiss

Design and illustrations by Paul Kepple and Scotty Reifsnyder @ Headcase Design
www.headcasedesign.com
Edited by Mindy Brown
Production management by John McGurk

Distributed in North America by Chronicle Books
680 Second Street
San Francisco, CA 94107

10 9 8 7 6 5 4 3 2 1

Quirk Books
215 Church Street
Philadelphia, PA 19106
www.quirkbooks.com

Contents

Congratulations!

And so now we get to the fun part—you get to plan a wedding! Woo hoo! Except . . . also, since you've got this book open, I might guess that "woo hoo" is not exactly how you're feeling about planning a wedding, huh? You've got questions. You've got concerns. You've got hives—not about marriage of course, or the wonderful man who's just invited you into it—but about planning this thing.

Never fear. It's going to be fine.

For starters, might I suggest not seeing this in a big-picture kind of way (as a huge undertaking), but rather that you try to think of each aspect of planning a wedding individually. It'll seem a lot less intimidating that way: You get to pick out pretty flowers! Eat good food! Shop for the prettiest dress you'll ever own! Because that's how we're going to manage it. We're going to take it one step at a time, and each task is going to be neatly finished and stashed away before you even realize it.

We're also going to go about this in an order that makes sense—in other words, you shouldn't need to skip ahead to find out how to accomplish the task that needs to get done next. We're going to make a few general decisions right off the bat, and those will be of the all-consuming type that will shape the way you get down to the nitty-gritty of planning your event. And if making these decisions gives you slight heart palpitations and makes you grab your hair with the subconscious intention of yanking it out, don't worry. They're big decisions, and unless you've been planning this day your entire life, it's completely normal not to know exactly what you want. Just rest assured that once you figure out the type of event you want, when you want it, how big it'll be, and what your overall budget looks like, moving forward should be nothing but a pleasant experience.

And what will the nitty-gritty be? Well, we've got to pick and book your vendors. Once you've done that, we get to have some of that aforementioned fun: Sampling yummy menus and deciding what you'd like to have served at your reception. Weighing your options between pale pink calla lilies and deep plum tulips. Dipping bites of chocolate cake, butter pound cake, or carrot cake into bowls of caramel, chocolate, and raspberry fillings and buttercream frostings to see which one you'd like to see on your spouse's nose at your reception. Selecting invitations in your favorite colors and counting up all the ecstatic "Yes!" replies you receive. And, lest we forget—picking out another pretty (and hopefully sparkly) ring.

If you ever feel yourself getting overwhelmed, take a step back. Go on a walk or a date with your husband-to-be, and don't talk or think about the wedding. Remember that there are no rules—no "hot" or "not" when it comes to what you do with your wedding—and that this day can be anything you want it to be. And although this day is certainly a biggie, it is just *one* day: What you're really preparing for is a wonderful lifetime married to the wonderful man of your dreams. No amount of unmatched table linens or drunken speeches is going to change the fact that at the end of the day, you will finally be husband and wife. So enjoy it!

[Chapter 1]

You're Enaged–
Now What?

You know that one-task-at-a-time thing we talked about? Here's where we start to break it down—and where you'll actually start thinking about things, deciding things, decreeing things, booking things. You get the idea.

Just remember, whenever you feel yourself getting overwhelmed, you're probably doing that big-picture thing again. Don't imagine your wedding date and work backward. We're only moving forward here.

Take 5 and Enjoy It!

I'm serious about this one. People are going to start asking you questions right away. As in, maybe even strangers who notice your ring while you're on your way to telling the people who actually know you:

- "Do you have a date yet?"
- "What are your colors?"
- "Where's it going to be?"
- "Is your third cousin twice removed on your step-dad's mother's side going to be your maid of honor?"

You're going to have to field wedding-related questions incessantly and immediately—but that doesn't mean you've got to have actual answers. Once it starts, it can be all-consuming at times, so take a minute here. Enjoy introducing your groom-to-be as your fiancé, spend hours on end staring at your ring, and take some time to enjoy your relationship as you've always known it. Soon, it'll be hard to talk to him without asking if he prefers the skewered tandoori shrimp or veal tips on toast. In other words, don't cave under the pressure of everyone's quest for information and feel like you've got to plan this thing starting now. You don't. You'll get there, all in due time.

Imagining Your Big Day: Setting Priorities

After your Take 5, there are just a few things you should get squared away, and then you can take another little chill pill. They're the biggest, or most basic, things you need to have set in order to plan everything else, and you'll feel a load lifted once you check them off your list.

■ **What time of year—or in what month—do you want to have your wedding?** This may seem like an easy answer to come by—and maybe, when it simply comes to your preference, it is—but it's one that may take some thinking. Maybe your whole life you've dreamed of a gorgeous September wedding, and you just can't imagine it any other way. Well, what if you are proposed to in February? You'll have to decide if you want to/can plan a wedding in seven months, or if you'd rather keep your preferred wedding time of year and wait a whole year and a half. If the latter seems like a long time and you'd really love just a simple celebration, do some digging. Talk to venues and vendors; it can probably be done. But if you want an extremely elaborate affair at the most sought-after place in town, it probably won't happen on a crash schedule.

■ **What type of event do you want?** This is another decision that is totally up to you and your groom. What are you envisioning when you imagine your first dance? Are you in a grand ballroom, at a swanky, chic, city-at-night

RUSTIC

DISCO

IMAGINING YOUR BIG DAY: Take time to decide the ideal type of

ELEGANT

SETTING W-DAY PRIORITIES:

1. Determine the time of year or month for your wedding

2. Plan the type of event you envision for your big day

3. Decide how many people can realistically attend

4. Determine whether all your Most Important People can travel to the wedding

wedding you and your groom would most enjoy with your friends and family.

type of affair? Do you see yourself in a rustic setting, in a high-ceilinged, whitewashed barn, with simple, organic décor? Decide before you head off making other decisions. It's going to affect the venue you choose, and ultimately the décor, the attire of you and your wedding party, and everything that goes along with it.

EXPERT TIP: Destination weddings. If, when you imagine your first dance, you picture the island in the Bahamas where you took your first real vacation together as a couple or that vineyard in Italy where your fiancé proposed, know that this sort of destination wedding is an entirely different animal. Even if you get that "That's it!" feeling when you envision beachside or Tuscan nuptials, you will need to decide: Can your budget handle this sort of event? Can your guests' budgets handle this sort of event? Do you care if lots of your guests' budgets cannot, in fact, handle this sort of event? Do you want to deal with planning this wedding via phone calls, e-mails, and wishing on a prayer that the florist your venue contact hooked you up with isn't just going to pluck a few hibiscus blooms from the front lobby, wrap a bow around them, and call it a day? If you decided you're willing to do whatever it takes to have your dream destination wedding, that's great—but do your homework, make calls, find out what paperwork needs to be filed where, sign on the assistance of a planning expert, and get all your ducks in a row before declaring yourself a destination bride.

■ **Can everyone you want to be there, be there?** While there are certain aspects of wedding planning that are simply unacceptable to conduct via e-mail, once you have an idea of when you think your wedding will be, you should check in with your Most Important People. Fire off a message to close family members and any and all potential wedding party members who simply must be there, and feel them out. You may not realize that two of your college roomies who happen to be cousins already have a family reunion in Boca Raton that weekend—and once you've signed contracts and shipped out real save-the-dates, it's too late. You'll be sorry you didn't check in with them before designing your stationery.

■ **What size of an event are you envisioning?** I bet you're thinking, "This is up to me, too." Kind of. (Unless you are paying for this celebration 100 percent yourselves, in which case, it is.) The size of your wedding celebration can be influenced by a variety of factors, the most likely having to do with the type of party you're going for, your venue, and your overall budget.

Determining Your Initial Budget

[1] **Make a preliminary guest list with your fiancé, to get on the same page.** When you picture your wedding, who do you see there? Is it truly just your closest family and friends? Or is it an all-out party, with everyone you've both ever known packing onto the dance floor until the DJ calls it quits and goes home? In either case, it's easy to underestimate how quickly people can add up.

[2] **Do your homework.** Maybe since you were a little girl, every time you've driven by a certain place—a beautiful marble ballroom, a gorgeous park with white swans swimming in a pond in the middle of it, the fanciest restaurant in the city—you've known *that's* where your wedding is going to be. That's where you want it; that's where you're going to have it; and their capacity is what is going to determine the size of your guest list. If you have any such special requirements, gather all the information, and of course, fill in your spouse-to-be. He may not realize the size of his wedding is in direct proportion to the fire codes of a particular ballroom.

[3] **Figure out your initial budget and who's paying for it.** In most cases, this is ultimately going to be what determines the size of your guest list. If, like many couples, you are receiving either financial aid or complete financial support from either set of parents, talk to them first about your budget. Because most venues—and caterers, and bakers, etc.—are going to quote you a price per person, the number of people you invite will directly influence that price:

(Venue + Menu) x Guest = $$

Think about it: If your wedding costs $200 a head, and you just throw your three co-workers and two of their spouses in there because you feel you *should* (lest it be awkward the first Monday back from your honeymoon), that's another $1,000 added to your total. Another $1,000 at the venue, and maybe you'll have to switch to a less expensive bloom in the centerpieces or the cheaper paper for your invitations. This is the way you've got to link your budget to the size of your wedding.

The other thing about other people paying and the size of your guest list has to do with the check-writers getting a say. Weren't expecting your mom's bridge partner and your dad's golf buddies to be there, clutching tissues while you and your beloved say your vows? If your parents are paying, and they want their guests to come, they'll probably be there.

Budget Cheat Sheet
Use this form to track all possible expenditures for your wedding day festivities.

OVERALL BUDGET AVAILABLE

	Venue	$
	Catering	$
	Photographer	$
	Dress	$
	Invitations	$
	Flowers	$
	Transportation	$
	Music	$
	Extras	$
	TOTAL	$

What Will Matter Most to Your *Overall* Budget?

Once you know who's filling the pot, be it yourselves, your parents, your fiancé's parents, or a trust from your great-grandfather, figure out your overall budget number before you start planning. You can't take any of the next steps without it.

Breaking down the specifics of your budget might have to come a little later. But mull things over.

■ If you know you want the best photographer in the state and his top-of-the-line package will eat up 40 percent of your entire budget, then determine that first and figure out the rest from there.

■ If all you care about is that you're able to get the dress that you want and not the next-best-thing, then go find that dress and figure out what you've got left over.

■ If you're not sure what tops your list, just take small steps into investigating the worlds of the dress, the food, the venue, the catering, the photography, the invitations, the band—and that will help you figure out what funds to allot where. This is not an objective thing, of course, so no book can explain your top priority for you. Use the budget sheet on the previous page as a starting point. (Additional sheets are in the appendix, pp. 210–11.)

To Engagement Party or Not to Engagement Party?

Here's another question that is really up to you—and, often, probably your mom and dad. Maybe you're so excited that your honey's popped the question that you can't wait until the wedding events to celebrate it with all your friends and family. Maybe Mom and Dad would love for their friends who haven't met your groom-to-be to meet him before the big day. Or, alternatively, perhaps the idea of tacking on another pre-wedding event to the list of inevitable showers, bachelor parties, and so on is most definitely not appealing to you, and you'd rather that everyone just buy you a drink the next time they run into you at a bar.

Any decision you make on this front is fine. There are no etiquette rules that say you should or should not formally throw a big engagement party—or that those who love you most can't throw one (or several) in your honor.

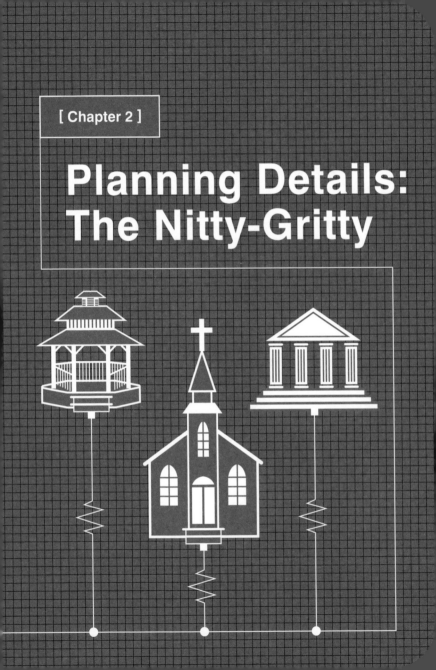

[Chapter 2]

Planning Details:
The Nitty-Gritty

You know what kind of affair you want, when you want it, (roughly) how big it is, and (roughly) what your overall budget is going to be. Now it's time to start making your first forays into the world of looking and booking. In this chapter, you'll check out reception venues and churches or synagogues, nail down your officiant, and, as a result, confirm your wedding date.

Now is also the time to think about anything (or anyone) else so important to you that it (or they) affect your choice of date. Often it will be the photographer who comes into play, since the good ones are in high demand and they can't be in two places at once on your wedding day (yours and the chick's who booked them a month before). But you may also find that the band is the focal point of your big day, and you absolutely must have your first choice locked in for your event. Now's the time to look into any of these "must-haves," check availability, and start signing people up. Each vendor will be dealt with in detail in the chapters that follow, but for the purposes of early planning stages, we'll first discuss venue with small teasers on choosing your photographer and officiant.

That Magical Site: Your Venue

This is a great time to use that fabulous tool modern brides are lucky to have at their fingertips: the Internet. Chances are, now that you've decided the type of place where you'd like to have your wedding, you're thinking of a few places in town where you should start looking.

VENUE POSSIBILITIES ARE ENDLESS

■ Go to their online sites. Google venues that meet your criteria in your area. Print out any info that pertains to you and your potential celebration: names of event coordinators at each place; catering packages; pictures of past weddings held there; capacity info for each scenario (cocktails, sit-down dinner, etc.).

■ Go through wedding magazines—preferably, *local* wedding magazines that highlight places specifically in your area.

■ Run down your mental list of weddings you may have attended in the area. Were any of the venues so memorable that you might consider the location for your own?

■ Once you've gathered all your little packets of printouts and magazines, grab your groom, spread the materials on the table in front of you, and start making calls to the sites that look good to you both.

■ Check for availability (some sites have online calendars) and set up appointments to visit in person. A lot of places will let you come in just as they've set up for a wedding, so you can get an idea of what it looks like once decorated, as opposed to an empty room with duct tape covering the wires on the floor.

■ If it's convenient for you, feel free to zip over to check out a site (church, ballroom, synagogue, hotel, park, etc.) on your lunch hour, even if it means going solo. Touring an entire site, top to bottom, accompanied by the site manager, can take a while—but if you just want to hit a bunch of places to narrow the field, go right ahead. If you are dazzled by a certain site but have to dart back to the office in time for your 3 o'clock meeting, simply sign up for a time on a Saturday when you can come back with a list of questions—and, of course, your groom.

Your Venue Research Checklist

While the event coordinator at each venue is leading you around, feel free to ask anything and everything you're wondering about that would affect your celebration.

■ **Does your celebration have to be over at a certain time?**

Some places, especially outdoor venues and those with strict town ordinances, might want you out by 9 P.M. If that doesn't work for you, you'll want to know this detail ahead of time. Also ask if the site is in a certain neighborhood that restricts noise (a.k.a. your rocking good time on the dance floor with the beautiful French doors that open onto the patio). If you're unwilling to sacrifice a kicking live band or a celebration that's partly outdoors, you'll want to know that up-front.

■ **Does each wedding package cover only a certain number of hours?**

Often, venues will tell you the latest hour at which your party is allowed to start—and even if you start before that, they only do five-hour celebrations. If you've got a rowdy crowd that tends to stay till the lights go off, they might feel squelched by such rules.

■ **What do you get with your package?**

- Does it cover all the food including the cake, or is the cake extra?
- Do they have an in-house caterer, an exclusive caterer, or a list of preferred caterers, or can you bring in whomever you like?
- If you want a vendor who's not on their list, do you have to pay an extra fee to have them do your wedding? Lots of hidden costs in venues lurk in the food area, so make sure you do some investigating.

■ **Is there a bride's room available for you and your wedding party?**

■ **How does parking work at the site?**

■ **Will the venue provide a point person?**

Will a catering manager or event coordinator be there to coordinate ven-

Venue Cheat Sheet

Use this sheet to record important details about the ven
compare impressions and information you've record

VENUE

Name		Date visited	☐☐ / ☐☐ / ☐☐

Address (Number and Street)	City

State/Province	Country	Zip/Postal Code

TEL ☐☐☐ – ☐☐☐ – ☐☐☐☐   Web site

COORDINATOR/MANAGER

MR. ○   MS. ○

TEL ☐☐☐ – ☐☐☐ – ☐☐☐☐   E-mail

Comments

_____

_____

_____

_____

_____

oices for your wedding. Once you've visited your top contenders, you can
each site.

CAPACITY

Ceremony	**Cocktails** ◯ YES ◯ NO
Dinner (seated)	**Dance floor**

Hours ☐☐ : ☐☐ — ☐☐ : ☐☐

CATERING

On-site	**Preferred list**
Fee, if bringing in own? $ ☐☐☐	**Includes cake** ◯ YES ◯ NO
Includes table and chairs ◯ YES ◯ NO	**Includes table linens** ◯ YES ◯ NO

EXTRAS

Site for photographs ◯ YES ◯ NO	**On-site Parking** ◯ YES ◯ NO
Restrictions	**Bridal Room**
Down Payment $ ☐☐☐	**Down Payment to Reserve** $ ☐☐☐

Overall Impressions

dors, light tea lights that go out, and do whatever needs to be done, without worrying the bride about it?

Once you've determined this information, be sure to take careful notes detailing what all of the venue costs (and any of its perks) will amount to. Hidden costs can add up, so the more transparent the information you receive, the better. Use the cheat sheet on the previous pages, and copy additional sheets from the appendix (pages 212–13).

EXPERT TIP: Be aware that, once you choose your venue, you will sign an official contract that spells out each of the issues outlined on your cheat sheet. Review this contract with great care to make certain that all of the issues agreed to are recorded in writing. Your venue will also ask for an up-front down payment to reserve the site, so be prepared with the proper amount when you sign your contract.

Venue? What Venue?

Maybe you don't dig ballrooms. Maybe there's not a museum in town that appeals to you, and you hate the beach. Maybe you've always dreamed of just a small, low-key, intimate ceremony and celebration in your parents' backyard or at the restaurant where you fell in love; or maybe the mutual friend who introduced you has a spread with a rolling backyard and a pool, and you'd like to say your vows—and then flip some burgers—around it. Great! Doing your wedding your way, at your own venue, will lend even more personal meaning to the day—not to mention, save you tons of legwork. Don't feel pressured into going the traditional route. You can determine the setting that means the most to you without slapping down a lot of cash.

Booking Your Photographer

Choosing a photographer is something that's good to get out of the way early, especially if photography is a high priority for you. Unlike a florist or catering company, which may be able to cover a few weddings on one day, a photographer will typically do only one event per day. This means they book up quickly—even more quickly if they're in high demand. You'll feel better during the planning process if you can rest assured that all the work you're doing will be beautifully and impeccably captured once it all falls into place. Further information about choosing the best photographer for you can be found on pages 80–88.

Booking Your Officiant

Perhaps you have an uncle who is a priest. Or you've been going to the same synagogue with the same rabbi since before you even knew your groom-to-be existed. Or your best friend is chomping at the bit to get ordained online so that she can tie your knot—after all, she introduced you.

If there is an officiant whose participation is significant to you, book him or her now. Most officiants—unlike your buddy who will get online certification, of course—can do only so many weddings per day, and they may need to arrange travel. Check in with them about your desired date, and book them as soon as you can get their commitment. Further details about choosing your officiant are on pages 166–68.

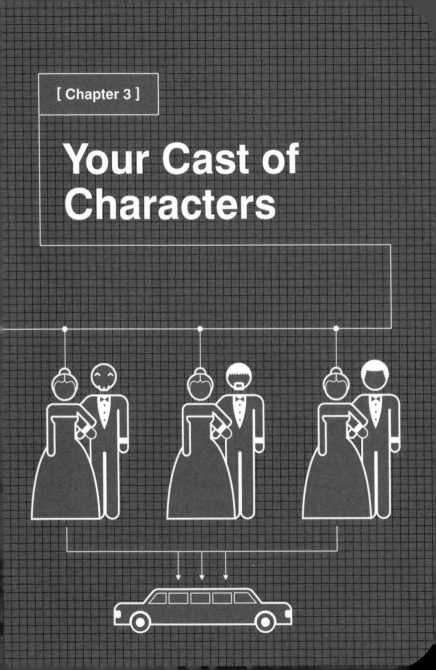

[Chapter 3]

Your Cast of Characters

Give yourself a pat on the back! You have a good chunk of the nitty-gritty details together, so you're well on your way. Now, who's going to stand up for you at your wedding, and who's going to be there to celebrate with you? Undoubtedly, very important decisions need to be made. But before you go about, in your bridal ecstasy, asking everyone on earth either to be in your wedding or to attend it, there are logistics to consider.

Selecting Your Attendants

These days, being in someone's wedding party is much more about the honor and privilege of standing up for your friend on one of the most important days of her life than it is a job with duties and responsibilities. So don't expect people to do your bidding. They'll call you Bridezilla, you'll find out, everyone will cry, and it'll be a big mess.

Attendants' Roles

Your attendants can, however, help with judicious favors here and there. These are the sorts of things you can ask them to do, and—if you've picked people who love you enough—they won't for one second hesitate to lend a helping hand.

[1] Your maid of honor can gather all the attendants' measurements.

[2] All your attendants can come to your place one night to drink wine and tie ribbons on 300 programs.

PROCEED WITH CAUTION WHEN PICKING BRIDESMAIDS

IMPORTANT DETAILS FOR CHOOSING ATTENDANTS:

1. Bridesmaid to groomsman ratio should be as close to balanced as possible.
2. Individual should be punctual for all wedding-related events.
3. Potential bridesmaids must be willing to pay for dresses.
4. Creative and fun personalities are key for planning festivities.

[3] With your mother or your fiancé's mother, they can throw a fabulous bridal shower for you and, if you like, one wild and crazy bachelorette party. (If they don't do this task at the very least, send them packing.)

Who Makes the Cut?

There will be a period of such sheer joy after your engagement that you're going to want to spread the love. That's fine—knock yourself out calling anyone you like to tell them of your engagement—just do not tack on, at the end of every conversation with your girlfriends or family members, that you'd love them to be a bridesmaid! Seriously. Just control yourself. Wait a few weeks and think about it.

■ **How many attendants do you really want up there with you?** It's likely that the women you want to be your bridesmaids will determine the number—i.e., you won't choose an arbitrary number and go from there, but rather assess the number of women who fit that role in your life.

■ **How many groomsmen will your groom have?** You'll want to have the two sides as close to balanced as possible.

Even though your attendants aren't necessarily going to have jobs to do, they do need to be reliable:

■ They have to show up on time to all wedding-related events.
■ They have to pay for their dresses.
■ They must have the wherewithal (and creativity, and fabulously fun instincts) to plan different events.

So think about each woman's reliability and how responsible she is. If you've got a friend who's going to drive you nuts throughout this process and maybe even end up in a totally different dress from the other five because she'll probably miss the deadline for ordering the one you picked, perhaps she could just do a reading at the ceremony.

Do pick your maid of honor with your eyes closed—as in, it should be that easy. Your maid of honor might be your sister (or both of your sisters, if you like!), your cousin who's like a sister, or that best friend who's been around forever. She's going to have a bit more to do than the others: She'll take the lead when it comes to planning pre-wedding parties, and if you need help with anything, she'll be the first one you ask. So while it's certainly important that she be able to handle all that, what's most important is that she's your number one girl.

Do not pick an attendant out of a feeling of (a) obligation or (b) guilt. Maybe you have a friend from college whom you talk to often but never planned to have in your wedding—yet she just asked you to be in hers. Maybe there's a woman you've been friends with for only two or three years, but she's been a great listener and has lots of time to help out. If these people wouldn't otherwise come to mind when you think of your bridesmaids, don't ask them to be in your wedding. It will be odd to have them standing up there with your sisters and the women with whom you've been best friends forever.

Do consider giving them other jobs or honors to show their special place in your life, such as doing a reading, being in charge of the guest book, or giving a toast.

In the end, pick the attendants who have always been there for you, and who will continue to be there for you through this process and the rest of your lives.

DRESSING THE PART:

1. Choose a gown everyone is comfortable wearing
2. Choose a gown that goes with colors of the season
3. Choose suits for a casual wedding and tails for a formal affair.

DRESSING YOUR ATTENDANTS: Here are a few helpful tips to keep

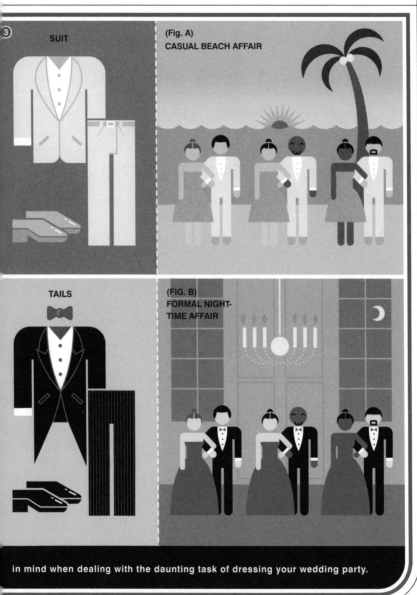

③ SUIT

(Fig. A)
CASUAL BEACH AFFAIR

TAILS

(FIG. B)
FORMAL NIGHT-TIME AFFAIR

in mind when dealing with the daunting task of dressing your wedding party.

Dressing Your Attendants

You know the drill. Your bridesmaids will desperately hope you'll pick out a dress for them that (a) looks friggin' *fantastic* on them, (b) costs oh, say, $50, and (c) is wearable to dressy events for years to come. Well, some of these things can happen, and some can't.

[1] When you're shopping for your bridesmaids' dresses (perhaps with one of them in tow, for modeling purposes), think about your color scheme. Try to pick a color that fits the season in which you're getting married and the palette you've chosen for your wedding flowers and other decor.

[2] Be kind—don't choose a style that's simply going to look awful on one of your attendants or that's going to make even one of them uncomfortable all night. You love them, right? Try to pick a universally flattering shape, and be sensitive about how much the dress costs.

[3] Finally, don't worry too much about whether your attendants can wear their dress again. They probably won't be able to, and deep down in their hearts, they know that. They can deal.

As for your groomsmen, try to do a similar thing: Choose a color and style that is appropriate for the wedding (khaki suits with white shirts and no tie are lovely for a casual beach wedding; long, formal tails look sharp for a formal, nighttime affair). These guys will almost surely be renting their getups, so the cost shouldn't be too much to worry about. They will, however, probably need to pick up the tie for whatever ensemble you choose. Let your groom have a say in this one—they're standing up for him, after all.

Devising Your Guest List

This, quite honestly, can be a doozie of a job. The good news: At least by now you already know the size of your guest list, as determined by your venue and the basic parameters of your budget. The less-good news: Now you've actually got to sit down and make The List.

Who Makes the Cut?

This seemingly simple task has the greatest potential to devolve into a group fight—ahem—*activity* than anything else you do while planning your wedding. It'll involve you, your parents, and your fiancé cross-checking his list with his parents. You'll start with a number bigger than the number of guests you can have and whittle it down from there.

Take nothing for granted: Even if you haven't spoken to your great Aunt Margaret who lives in Oregon since you were 11, your mother might insist upon her being invited. So use this time to find out what everybody's expectations are concerning who they'd like to invite.

[1] Write down the maximum capacity of your venue.

[2] Determine the number of "nonnegotiable" people you and your fiancé simply must have at your wedding.

[3] Determine the number of slots up for grabs by subtracting #2 above from #1.

[4] Tell both sets of parents that they have a remaining number of slots available for guests of their choosing. Either sit down with them and slot in

guests individually or simply give each set of parents an equal number of invites to do with as they see fit.

This group approach is of the utmost importance to your sanity—not to mention that of your stationer and your caterer.

This is also the time to decide what is perhaps one of the biggest details your guests will notice upon opening their mailbox: Who is going to be invited to bring a date? Typically, those with spouses, fiancés, or live-in or long-term (over a year in the same relationship, say) significant others get a date; others do not. Decide this issue across the board—and don't make exceptions—otherwise, you'll hear about it.

Finally, it's time to think about kids. Yes, we all enjoy the munchkins when they're cuddling on your lap or playing a silly tea party—but for your wedding day you've got to decide whether you (a) want them there and (b) can afford to have them there. Both questions should be pretty easy to answer.

■ If, right off the bat, you know you'd have to invite 35 kids, and you just can't eat up that much of your guest list or budget with pint-sizers, then your answer's probably "no kids."

■ If you know you want this day to be elegant and grown-up, and just not the type of affair where ketchup from the chicken finger platter could ever make its way onto your dress, then your answer, again, is "no kids."

■ On the other hand, if you've got four nieces and nephews, your fiancé's college roomie has twins, you love them all, and can't imagine the dance floor without them, then by all means include kids (although you may want to limit the number to close friends and relatives, depending on budget and circumstances).

⚠ **EXPERT TIP:** *People won't be furious with you if they had to hire a babysitter for the day, but your niece is front and center at the wedding. Kids in your immediate family get a free pass.*

Troubleshooting Sticky Issues

I don't mean to terrify you, but the behavior of your guests between the day they hear you're getting married and the moment they arrive at your wedding can be quite shocking. You may also realize you've made a few iffy decisions regarding the people you've invited. (The exciting extravaganza of paper products, colors, scripts and wording for said invitations is detailed on pages 138–44.) Here are a few examples of the problems that can arise after your invitations are sent—and how to handle them.

■ **People assume they're invited—oops.** Perhaps your mother-in-law's friend at work has sent you a lovely gift—along with a note saying how excited she is about the wedding. And, well, you're not inviting people you've never met. What to do? Have your mother-in-law explain that while she would love to have all her friends there, due to the size of the venue you're actually keeping the wedding small, and sadly no one from her office will be invited. Alternatively, send her a note to say thanks, and explain the situation yourself.

■ **People RSVP with a date—and they weren't invited with one.** Most people these days understand that if an invitation is addressed solely to them (as opposed to them "and Guest"), then they are the only guest invited. If you, however, are so lucky as to have invited guests who either aren't aware of that piece of etiquette or simply cheerfully disregard it, then you've got trouble. You will need to explain that your budget and/or venue can't

Drafting the Guest List

After you decide how many nonnegotiable guests will attend[ ]for potential "B" List Guests.

"A" LIST GUESTS

(A) TOTAL GUEST CAPACITY		TOTAL [ ][ ][ ]

(B) NONNEGOTIABLE GUESTS		

BRIDE'S	🧬 Family		[ ][ ][ ]
	❤️ Friends		[ ][ ][ ]
GROOM'S	🧬 Family		[ ][ ][ ]
	❤️ Friends		[ ][ ][ ]
CHILDREN INVITED		◯ Y ◯ N	[ ][ ][ ]

Add up all nonnegotiable guests	TOTAL [ ][ ][ ]

$$ (A) - (B) = (C) $$

(C) SEATING AVAILABLE FOR FOR "B" LIST GUESTS & RISKY INVITEES	TOTAL [ ][ ][ ]

e chart below will help you determine how many slots you have available

BRIDE AND GROOM'S "B" LIST GUESTS

Her Friends				His Friends			
Her Co-Worker(s)				His Co-worker(s)			
Her Boss				His Boss			
TOTAL				TOTAL			

PARENTS' "B" LIST GUESTS

	BRIDE'S PARENTS					GROOM'S PARENTS			
	Distant Relatives					Distant Relatives			
	Friends					Friends			
	Boss/Co-Workers					Boss/Co-Workers			
	TOTAL					TOTAL			

⚠ RISKY INVITEES *(consider carefully before inviting)*

◯ Divorced Friends ◯ him ◯ her	◯ Tipsy McSwagger
◯ Bride's Ex	◯ Troublemakers
◯ Groom's Ex	◯ Misc.

accommodate extra people not originally accounted for. (Depending on who the guest is, this may be a task your mother or planner can take on.) Of course, if you're fine with their addition, you may decide to let it slide—but just remember: You'll have to let all such offenders slide, as well.

■ **People refer to their children being excited about the party—and it's an adults-only reception.** People may not like this—and might even end up not coming as a result—but you've got to call them and explain that you're not having children at the reception. Blame it on your caterer charging a full head for their teeny portions or whatever, but you've got to maintain consistency across the board. If you let even one couple with kids through just to avoid an awkward conversation, you're going to anger people who read the invitation correctly (unless it says "and family," kiddies aren't included) and shelled out the coin for a babysitter. If you want to help out all your guests who have young children, you could arrange to have a babysitter available in the hotel where most of your guests are staying or at someone's house nearby—in which case, no one could accuse of you of not being accommodating.

■ **Some good friends are divorced—and they each ask if the other is coming.** Tell both friends that you hope they can come, but that you'll understand if they'd like to bow out gracefully (especially in lieu of making a scene at the open bar). And if they both RSVP yes, be happy you have such mature guests—and then seat them on opposite sides of the room.

■ **You were super organized and sent all your invitations in a timely manner, but the RSVP date has come and gone—without responses from several guests.** Most of the time, any MIA responses fall into two categories: (1) Close friends and family members who know you know they're coming and got lazy with their RSVP cards; or (2) people you never really thought would come (your friend from grade school who lives 400 miles away and is due with her third the day before your wedding), but whom you wanted to give the courtesy of being invited anyway. Guests in both categories—as well as people you just plain haven't heard from—will have to be called for a response. Do it yourself, or employ your mom or a wedding planner, but you (and your caterer) will need to know a definite head count. Most of the time, your tardy guests will gasp with embarrassment and apologies, saying they were waiting on just one little thing in their schedule to determine whether they could come.

■ **You didn't get back the number of RSVPs you expected—and you'd like to send out a second round.** Ah, the A-list/B-list scenario. Risky. Very risky. But it can be done. First, you've got to make sure you time it just right. If your first RSVP date is right before your final head count is due to your venue and caterer, the RSVP date for the second round is going to be, oh, about two days after they get the invite, and the jig will be up. Make sure you have enough time to get in the second round by the time you need to hand over your numbers, and you'll be OK. But remember: You can't just scatter people from the same "groups" across your A and B lists. You've got to compartmentalize. Put all your and your groom's co-workers in the second round, then seat them at the same tables. You can't invite some in each round, then dot them throughout your seating chart—you'll be found out in a heartbeat. Etiquette-wise, this isn't the taboo practice it once was, but try to treat people the way you'd like to be treated (which is to say, in such a way that they never find out they're on the B list).

■ **Your darling groom asks if "she" should be invited.** This is entirely up to you and your graciousness. And maybe whether your fiancé could stand having "him" around as well.

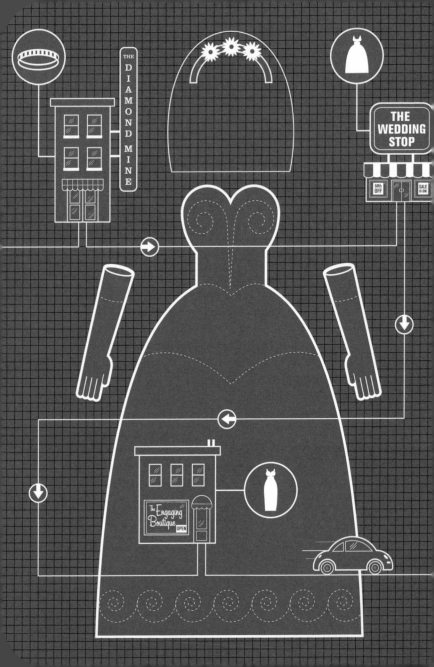

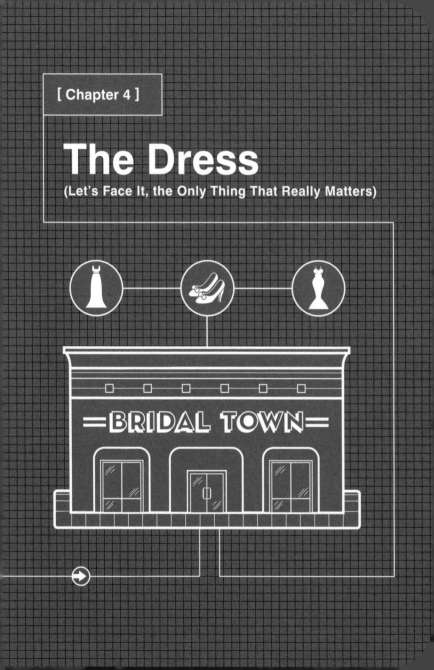

[Chapter 4]

The Dress
(Let's Face It, the Only Thing That Really Matters)

=BRIDAL TOWN=

After the rock is on your hand, and you've taken care of the things that need immediate attention (setting the date and booking the ceremony and reception sites, possibly the photographer if you know you want one who's in high demand, etc.), it's time to check off the one thing on your list that's probably been at the center of your wedding fantasies since you fastened a pillow case to your head as a girl and ran about the house singing "Here Comes the Bride."

The Dress. Ah, the Dress.

Shopping for the Dress

Although we realize it *should* be the most fun item to cross off your list, you really do need to get started early. Special ordering, customizing anything, and having the gown arrive in enough time to alter it during the various stages of your inevitable pre-wedding diet take a lot of time—preferably nine months to one year before you walk down the aisle. So let's get shopping!

EXPERT TIP: Before the Scouting Mission. While thinking about monetary restrictions may momentarily rain on your shopping parade, make sure you put together some sort of budget before engaging in a full-on frenzy. Figure out a numeric value and stick to it. Don't even try on a dress that is excessively over your budget: You may fall in love with it, and if your budget makes owning it impossible, you will look upon the dress you do purchase with resentment and, possibly, disdain. This is not how brides should feel about their dress. Don't let it happen to you.

The Look Book

If you're not quite sure what kind of dress you want, and have not been fantasizing about your wedding dress since grade school, make a "look book" prior to shopping:

[1] Rip out pages from magazines, print out pictures from designers' Web sites, steal from your best friend's wedding album—basically, when you see a dress you like, cut it out and paste it in a little scrapbook of potential dresses.

[2] Study the images of different looks to help you determine the patterns of things you do and do not like. This will make it much easier to communicate what you're looking for to the bridal salon staff.

[3] Make a note of what it is you like about each dress:
- Is it the material?
- The structure?
- The cut?

Just remember that the dresses you're looking at are probably on gazelle-like models, and unless you are frequently mistaken for Gisele (in which case, pardon us), you may end up honing your ideas only once you start to see things fitted to you.

Picking Your Shopping Entourage

There is no pressure to find *the* dress—or any dress—on your first shopping mission. You may even want to visit a few shops and see what's out there before you decide where you'd like to make appoint-

ments for try-ons. You can make this trip alone, or you may want to bring a trusted friend with tastes similar to yours.

When you decide you'd like to actually brave the world of try-ons, think about whom you'd like to have with you. You're about to see yourself in a wedding dress for the first time, and you may be surprised at how emotional you become. That said, don't feel that you need to have your entire bridal party or your entire extended family with you to witness this magical moment. Ask yourself:

- Who would be helpful to have around while you're trying to make a hard decision?
- Do your mom, sister, and best friend keep you grounded?
- Will they be honest when it comes to weighing your options?
- Will they *tell* you if they can see your cellulite through that sheath or if that strapless really plays up just how flat as a board you are?

If so, bring them.

- Do you have one friend who's not necessarily your closest but is just really helpful when you start feeling overwhelmed?

If so, bring her.

On the other hand, if your mother's harping makes you break out in hives all over your chest—which would undoubtedly make it hard to tell whether you like a sweetheart or V-neck neckline—wait until you've narrowed it to two or three dresses before asking her to come along to offer an opinion. This trip doesn't have to be a party; simply bring someone or some people who will be fun and helpful.

Grazing

Looking at racks and racks of dresses, especially dresses in all the same color, can be very overwhelming.

[1] Approach them with an open mind. If you see something you like—or even *think* you might like—try it on. Don't let the way a dress looks on a hanger make you hesitate to try it. Hangers can make dresses appear much different from how they look on your body.

[2] Be aware that there are trends in the bridal fashion industry each season. Designers may decide, from time to time, that they like heavy beading or excessively long trains of chiffon. But while this may influence the selection of dresses available in the stores, it won't limit the variety, and it shouldn't cause you to purchase a style that's different from the one you've envisioned.

[3] Try on as many as you like, and even if that first one makes you gasp, makes everyone around you weep, and makes all the salon consultants gather around and shake their heads in wide-eyed wonder—don't be too quick to pull out your credit card. There may be another dress out there that gets an even stronger reaction.

[4] This is not to say that you need to try on hundreds of dresses (as a matter of fact, *don't*), but it will pay to look around and compare and contrast. When you find one that you keep coming back to no matter what you put on or where you go, well then, chances are you've found The Dress.

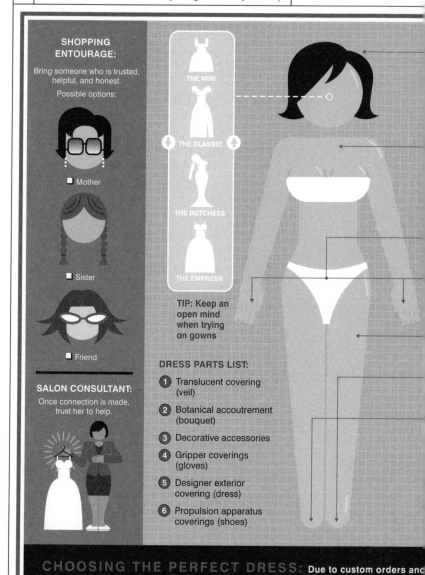

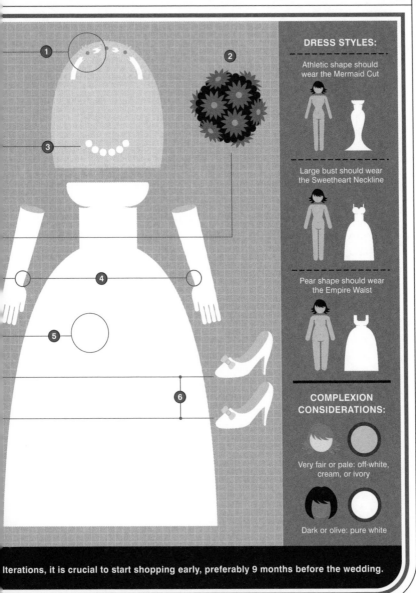

1

2

3

4

5

6

DRESS STYLES:

Athletic shape should wear the Mermaid Cut

Large bust should wear the Sweetheart Neckline

Pear shape should wear the Empire Waist

COMPLEXION CONSIDERATIONS:

Very fair or pale: off-white, cream, or ivory

Dark or olive: pure white

Iterations, it is crucial to start shopping early, preferably 9 months before the wedding.

Dealing with Wedding Dress Consultants

Salon consultants are there to help you find your wedding dress. Period. Acquaint yourselves before you start tossing dresses into your fitting room.

■ Tell her about the type of wedding you're having, highlighting anything unusual about the setting (if it's on the beach, outside, etc.), and talk about your body concerns and the styles you like.

■ If you feel she's not interested and just seems like she's there to make the sale, ask if there is another consultant you can talk to. Your consultant needs to understand where you're coming from if she's going to help you find the perfect dress. If she doesn't have a feel for your style, she's going to be about as helpful in that capacity as your Labrador Retriever.

■ Once you've made a connection with your consultant, trust her: If she brings you a dress with an empire waist, try it on—even if you've already told her you want a dropwaist. She does this for a living and has seen a thousand brides with your physical characteristics. She may have noticed that you have lovely shoulders, or really narrow hips, or a shorter-than-average torso, and she'll bring you dresses that she's seen look gorgeous on women with bodies like yours. After all, it's not about finding the exact dress that you've always *thought* you wanted; it's about finding the dress that looks the most fabulous when it's actually on you.

For Your Consideration: A Glossary of Terms

As you graze the racks, think about how the color and cut of each dress will look on your body. Here are some general characteristics to think about. These are not hard-and-fast rules, of course—merely helpful generalizations that have evolved over years of brides-to-be having nervous breakdowns in fitting rooms.

Complexion

You may feel free to try on a dress of any shade, but if you are frustrated by how you look in certain hues, there's probably a reason. As a general rule, girls who are fair or pale tend to look better in off-white, ivory, or cream—colors that won't wash out their light complexions. In recent years, bridal designers have even begun making beautiful dresses in shades of Champagne and pale pink, which are also flattering. (Go ahead, give 'em a whirl. No one's going to whisper about why you're not wearing white.) Women with dark or olive skin tones look stunning in pure white because it forms a lovely contrast.

Body Type

Weight and body type are two different things. Weight has the potential to change throughout your life, and especially during the wedding-planning process. Your body type is the stuff that just is—the shape your mother and grandmothers have bestowed upon you that can't be changed by squats or pushups or miles on the treadmill.

For example, if you are tiny or petite, chances are a princess or full ball-gown style is going to swallow you up in layers of tulle. If your dress weighs more than you, each bathroom trip you take at your wedding will interrupt the good time being had by your bridesmaids, who will have to come with you to hold it up. Use the guidelines in the following glossary to determine the best styles for your body type.

Knowing the names of the cuts, hems, shapes, and silhouettes you prefer will help you communicate with consultants to get the dress you want. Added bonus: You'll sound like you know what you're talking about *and* be able to engage in bridal fashion-savvy banter with other passing brides.

Gown Silhouettes

■ **The A-line**. This classic shape can be strapless or not; it's fitted around the bust and waist, with the fabric then flowing outward and to the ground in a shape that loosely resembles an uppercase A.
Who should wear this style: Universally flattering (even in white), it is a very popular and common design.

■ **Mermaid cut.** This style is usually strapless, fitted through the bust, torso, hips, and buttocks, and flaring out right above the knees.
Who should wear this style: If you're athletic, have a tiny frame, or a great shape you'd like to show off, try it on—this look is sexy. Not too thrilled about those particular fitted areas? Keep looking.

■ **Full Princess/Ball.** This shape is fundamentally an A-line cut on steroids. The gown is fitted through the bust and waist and then poufs out and to the ground (in various stages of poufiness, depending on the number of layers of pouf-inducing material, such as tulle, taffeta, organza, or crinoline).

Who should wear this style: An excellent look for pear-shaped women, as it accentuates a small waist and hides a heavier lower body; it's perfect also if you've always wanted a fairy-tale wedding (or to be a princess). But if you're teeny or have a fuller figure, you should keep looking. You don't want to be overwhelmed by the pouf or unfavorably enhanced by it.

■ **Empire.** With this look, the waist begins right beneath the bust, and the fabric flows freely from there to the ground. The dress may be strapless or not. This style can lend a lovely Grecian-goddess feel to your look.

Who should wear this style: This very fluid look is friendly to every body type—especially those who would like to hide troublesome features south of the bust. It's nicely suited for a small bust, as it draws eyes to the neckline and a lovely collarbone. Women with a large bust will find that they feel controlled and confined in this cut.

■ **Column/Sheath.** This stunning shape has a simple, classic line that runs from top to toe without any breaks. *Who should wear this style:* If you are long and lean, this is the look for you. However, if you have any problem areas you'd like to conceal—*anywhere* on your body—keep looking. This shape tends to be clingy, and some styles can be constricting, thereby impeding your ability to sit, dance, eat, or *breathe* as comfortably as you'd like on your wedding day.

Necklines

■ **Standard strapless.** With this classic look, the top of the dress cuts across the chest, usually with a soft arc, from armpit to armpit.
Who should wear this style: A flattering look for many body types but especially for anyone with toned arms—the horizontal line draws the eye to your shoulders and upper arms.

■ **Square neck.** With this look, the neckline cuts straight across the chest to meet the straps (usually thicker than spaghetti width) at a 90-degree angle. The square neck can also be employed for sleeveless gowns or dresses with long, flowy sleeves.
Who should wear this style: Flattering for all body types.

■ **Sweetheart neckline.** The best way to imagine this style is to picture the top of a heart. Instead of cutting straight across the chest, the neckline has two semicircle curves above the bodice.

Who should wear this style: This line can be very flattering on larger-busted women who want to feel supported and not like they're about to flash their guests.

■ **V Neck.** This is a shape you'll be familiar with from your favorite old T-shirt. Sheath dresses often are designed with a V neck, in which the line of the dress plunges down the middle of the chest from the shoulders.

Who should wear this style: Suitable for most body types. If you have a large bust, go with a high V, so as not to flash your officiant. If you've got a smaller bust, you can get away with a low V.

■ **Scoop neck.** The neckline has a soft downward curve, much like the shape of a "U," and it can be as low or as high as you like, much like the V neck.

Who should wear this style: Most women can pull off a scoop neck no matter what their shape.

■ **Halter neck.** This is another shape you probably already have in your closet—in your stash of shirts for going out on the town. Halters can be scoop neck or V neck; as the straps come up to the shoulders, they wrap behind the neck.

Who should wear this style: You had better be in love with your neck and shoulders (not to mention the entire length of your arms), because that's where everyone will be looking.

Sleeves

■ **Cap sleeves.** Teeny-tiny mini sleeves that hug the top of your shoulder. These lend a romantic look to the dress, so you'll often find that they are lacy or sheer, in contrast to the rest of the dress.

Who should wear this style: Brave this look only if you have toned or slim arms.

■ **Illusion sleeves.** Long sleeves that travel to the wrist and are made of transparent material. This is a lovely place on your dress for a bit of embellishment with beading or crystals.

Who should wear this style: Anyone wishing for a bit more coverage while still showing off the arms.

Trains and Veils

■ **Blusher. (1)** This veil comes to just beneath your chin, or the top of your chest, and can be combined with a longer veil for a more dramatic look.
Who should wear this style: A useful veil if you wish to wear it over your face during the procession and then flip it to the back of your head during the ceremony.

■ **Chapel. (2)** This veil flows down the back of your dress, just over your train.
Who should wear this style: Anyone having a more formal wedding.

■ **Cathedral. (3)** This veil extends beyond your train for an even more formal look.
Who should wear this style: If you want to make an extra-dramatic entrance, this is the veil to go with—though make sure you've picked an equally dramatic dress that can stand up to it.

■ **Mantilla. (4)** This Spanish-influenced veil drapes just over the head (not the face) and usually has a scalloped edge trimmed in lace.
Who should wear this style: A mantilla can add a lovely and unexpected look to any style of dress. It's also quite a flexible look because you can find a mantilla veil in any length you'd like.

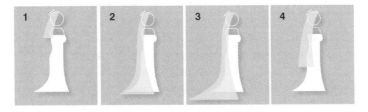

Other Bridal Fashion Accoutrements

In the excitement over choosing your dress, try not to forget about everything else you'll need to go with it—it's not the only thing you'll be wearing that day, after all. As soon as you've got your dress (or at least before it comes in), shop for undergarments and proper shoes. In order for the seamstress to fit you correctly each and every time you show up for a fitting minus another 4 pounds, you'll need to wear the exact same underthings and shoes as you'll be wearing on your big day. What you wear under your dress will have everything to do with the shape and cut of your dress—especially the neckline. And, no matter what that may be, you can find something out there to support and flatter you in that shape.

■ A good white or nude seamless bustier is usually a never-fail go-to for brides, but talk with the associates at your favorite lingerie shop. They will help you find the perfect bra for your needs.

■ Bring your bustier or bra to your dress fitting so there won't be any surprises on your wedding day, when you find there's not even a millimeter's room left for a silky smooth layer of satin.

Shoes are entirely up to you. Love slingbacks? Strappy sandals? Sky-high heels? Kitten ones? Indulge yourself. And if you can, bring a swatch of your dress while shoe shopping, or buy your shoes in the same shop as where you got your dress, to make sure you're perfectly coordinated.

Expert Tip: Once you've picked your dress, work with both the salon consultant who helped you choose your dress and the hair salon consultant who will be doing your 'do on your wedding day. The former will make sure your veil or headpiece coordinates with your gown, and the latter will make sure that whatever you're wearing on your head works with your hairdo.

Don't Forget the Rings!

We realize that you may still be in a tizzy about your engagement ring. It's sparkly, it's pretty—maybe it's huge—and it reminds you every time you look at it that someone asked you to spend the rest of your life with him. It's all you ever wanted from the second you met.

So go ahead and tizzy away—but don't forget about your wedding bands. Those are the symbols of eternity that you'll *both* wear for the rest of your lives: the circle, the union, the promise that never ends. So don't shortchange your bands.

Whatever you have planned (or don't have planned) for your bands, give yourself two to three months from your wedding day, at least, to start shopping. That way, if you don't find something you like and want/need to get something custom-made—even if it's just ordering a different size or tweaking a design—you won't be overly rushed. Forever is a long time, after all. You don't want to fly through the process and *then* wish you'd had time to get that gorgeous filigree pattern engraved onto your band.

Start out looking at rings at the jeweler who carried your engagement ring. Alternatively, go to a jeweler whom you know and like—preferably one you or your family has gone to over the years—and who will be disposed to give you a good deal. If neither is an option, simply pick a store that carries designers you're interested in or that has a good reputation in your area. While browsing, here are some factors to consider:

■ **The Metal.** You probably already know if you want your metal to be white or yellow (i.e., whatever your engagement ring is). Talk to your jeweler about the pros and cons of gold. It's an extremely soft metal, and depending on the design and what sorts of activities you spend your day doing, your ring could get knocked around a lot. If you choose platinum—increasingly the most popular bridal metal, and among the most durable—be prepared for a price increase, and maybe having to sacrifice some bling in order to get it.

■ **Style.** Maybe there's a band that was made to go with your engagement ring, and you love that. Maybe all you want is a solid, plain ring. Or maybe you've got pictures from magazines or your grandmother's old ring—some very specific design that you're setting out to find or have made, come hell or high prices. Browse the store and talk to your jeweler. Usually, any design can be made—you simply need to figure out budgeting and timing.

■ **Stones.** This is, of course, another area that's completely up to you and your wallet. There are millions of options out there, whether you want just a teeny diamond imbedded into the band, some pavé work, or a whole eternity band of diamonds. Try on a bunch—you'll need to make sure the band complements your engagement ring without competing or overwhelming it.

As for your groom's ring, be prepared for him to wince a bit. He may have never worn jewelry, and although he cannot *wait* to marry you, he hasn't really settled on the idea of having a *thing* on his finger for the rest of his life. So don't get too frustrated with him. Go through all the options just as the two of you do for your ring, looking at plain styles and shapes that are comfortable to him and that flatter his lovely, manly hand.

Once you've purchased your rings, make sure to get specific instructions from your jeweler or the designer on how to care for them. It's the most important piece of jewelry you'll ever wear, and you'll want to take every precaution so that it doesn't get lost (finding the perfect fit) or damaged (learn how to spot a loose stone and how often to get that nicked-up gold band buffed smooth).

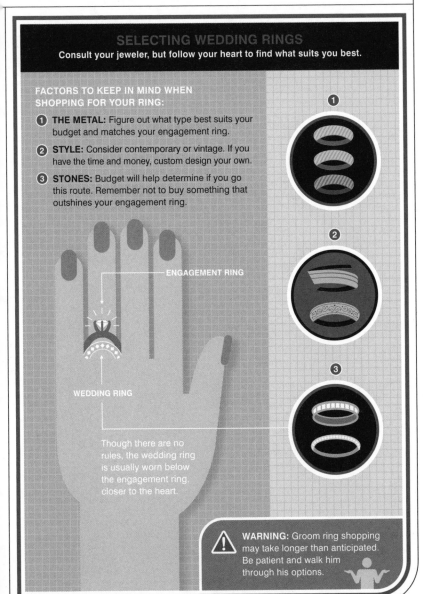

SELECTING WEDDING RINGS
Consult your jeweler, but follow your heart to find what suits you best.

FACTORS TO KEEP IN MIND WHEN SHOPPING FOR YOUR RING:

1 **THE METAL:** Figure out what type best suits your budget and matches your engagement ring.

2 **STYLE:** Consider contemporary or vintage. If you have the time and money, custom design your own.

3 **STONES:** Budget will help determine if you go this route. Remember not to buy something that outshines your engagement ring.

ENGAGEMENT RING

WEDDING RING

Though there are no rules, the wedding ring is usually worn below the engagement ring, closer to the heart.

WARNING: Groom ring shopping may take longer than anticipated. Be patient and walk him through his options.

Chapter 5

Casting Your Wedding Day

THE PHOTOGRAPHER

THE WEDDING PLANNER

THE FLORIST

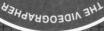

THE VIDEOGRAPHER

And now it's time to turn to the people who are actually going to execute many of the details throughout your wedding day: your wedding planner, your photographer (and videographer), and your florist. These people are vitally important—almost as important as the bride and the groom (*almost*)—because each vendor is responsible for an integral part of the day. And you and your fiancé no doubt already have some ideas about just how big a role each of these will play in your day, so get ready to hone your decision-making skills about what is and isn't important to you. (Just remember, this is excellent practice for your life as a married couple.)

You will want to entrust each vendor with managing all the details so that you can be focused on enjoying yourself. Make no mistake: These are not the types of roles you can fill by simply opening the yellow pages, closing your eyes, and pointing.

[1] Do a little research before you begin calling around. Search the Web for local vendors' sites and buy local wedding magazines that showcase the work of the vendors in your area.

[2] Take notes as you go, jotting down ideas you like and the people who provide the services you need.

[3] Narrow your candidates to a few, then call and set up face-to-face meetings, preferably in their studio or business.

[4] During your consultation, tell the vendor the general size and scope of your wedding, so you'll not only get a monetary estimate of their basic services, but also be able to tell whether you "click" with them.

And, FYI, you *have* to click with them. If you think they're snotty or they think you're high-maintenance, this will not make for a very pretty or low-stress planning situation. If you can tell you're just not that into them, or they're just not that into you and your ideas, keep looking. If the vendor is someone with whom you immediately feel a rapport, and with whom you can see yourself having a friendly give-and-take throughout the process, keep them high on your list. Clicking is just as important as how nicely they can tie a bouquet or put together a dinner menu.

[5] Once you've made your choices, be prepared to complete a written contract with each vendor. Read this contract. Ask questions. Request changes and additions. Be aware that the fine print can contain surprises, hidden costs, and if-this-then-that scenarios you'll need to assess before signing and proceeding with their services.

The Wedding Planner

Your wedding planner will be your savior from the very beginning of the planning process up to the minute you board your honeymoon plane. Or she may be present only on the wedding day, arriving on the scene to make sure all goes smoothly—and that you are blissfully unaware if it doesn't.

To (Professionally) Plan or Not to (Professionally) Plan?

This is the first question you've got to figure out—and whether or not your budget can even accommodate such a service is usually pretty easy to answer. It's a financial and personal decision that is best

reached after discussion with your spouse-to-be and your gracious financiers.

If your budget can afford it, here are some of the indispensable services your planner will provide:

■ High-level assistance when it comes to wrangling, selecting, and hiring each of your vendors;

■ A cohesive theme that's evident from the first save-the-date card that goes out until the last favor is given away on your wedding night;

■ Detail work devoted to managing phone calls and setting up meetings on your behalf;

■ And most important, the assurance that someone is there on the day of your wedding to coordinate everything and everyone, be in charge, and put out fires without your ever lifting a finger or even having to ask someone else to lift a finger.

If that last point sounds especially appealing, and a day-of planner/wrangler is all you can afford, go for it. You'll probably find that it's worth it. But if you simply don't have room for a wedding planner in your budget at all—or you simply don't mind taking care of all this stuff on your own or with the help of trusted friends—that's fine, too. You'll need to take extra care, as the date nears, that each of your vendors is on top of his or her game and aware of what the others are doing and when on the big day.

Selecting a Wedding Planner

If you've decided to go with a planner, make sure to choose one who will provide the precise services you need. Confirm, for example, that they'll do just the day-of, if that's all you want or can afford. When interviewing a planner, ask the following questions:

- Have you ever worked at [venue] before?
- How do you charge for your services? Do you have packages?
- Would I be able to talk to a bride whose wedding you've planned?
- Do you tend to always work with the same florists, bakers, etc., or are you familiar with a wide circle of area vendors (and can you help me narrow down the list)?
- How many times will we meet throughout the wedding process? Is this a team event, or do I just tell you what I want and you'll take off running?

You'll work with your planner more than any of your other vendors, so you'll want her to be a sure thing by the time you sign. Talk to the manager at the venue you've chosen to make sure your planner has a good track record of working at the site. Also be sure to talk to brides who've used the planner's services before. You'll be glad to ask a bride who's actually used the planner's services about the nitty-gritty questions you'd like to know. (Are they bad at answering e-mail, but always answer their cell phone? Did the planner ever let you down or steer you wrong?) Such first-hand knowledge is invaluable. Use the sheet on the following pages to record pertinent information. (Additional sheets can be copied from the appendix, pages 216–17.)

Wedding Planner Cheat Sheet

Use this sheet to help choose your wedding planner. Once you

WEDDING PLANNER

MR. ◯ MS. ◯

Interview:

DATE ☐☐ / ☐☐ / ☐☐   TIME ☐☐ : ☐☐   ◯ A.M. ◯ P.M.

Address (Number and Street)   City

State/Province   Country   Zip/Postal Code

TEL ☐☐☐ - ☐☐☐ - ☐☐☐☐   ◯ HOME ◯ WORK ◯ CELL ◯ FAX

Web site   Familiar with venue   ◯ YES ◯ NO

Package includes   Price $ ☐☐☐☐☐

We clicked/didn't click

de your choice, keep his or her contact information close to hand at all times.

PRIME DIRECTIVES

1. Analyze nuptial requirements
2. Integrate vendors
3. Manage meltdowns
4. Charge a lot of money

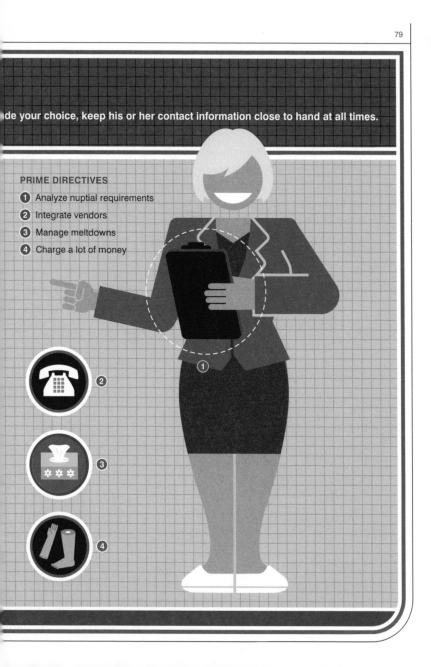

The Photographer

Your photographer is the person responsible for the oohing and ahhing over your wedding photos for years to come—i.e., eternity. Great-great-great-grandchildren you will never meet will look at the photos this person documents and exclaim what a lovely day you had.

When choosing this very important vendor, it's especially helpful to speak with someone who's used their services for her own wedding. But do so only after you've narrowed your list of candidates through a bit of research. You can get some initial referrals through friends who loved their own wedding photographers (or friends whose photos you've loved), from venue managers who've worked with many photographers and know which ones have worked well at their venues, and from wedding magazines that feature local photographers.

Peruse professional photographers' Web sites and the wedding magazines to study the photos they take.

- Do you like their style?
- Do they seem to have captured the kinds of moments you want to capture?
- Do they take all pictures in color? Some black and white and sepia?
- Do all their weddings seem to have the same shot, just with different players?
- Are there a gazillion traditional portraits, and you're not interested in posing for much of anything on your wedding day?

You'll find it's easier than you think to pick out photographers whose work really strikes a chord with you. You might even find yourself tearing up at wedding pictures consisting entirely of people you've never met. This might seem like a crazy reaction, but just imagine how you'll feel when they're pictures of *your* wedding.

Selecting a Style—Traditional vs. Photojournalistic

Most photographers will tell you that their style is unique, a combination of this and that, but there are two main categories into which all photographers' work will fall.

Traditional

Most simply put, a traditional wedding photographer will spend time having you pose, taking portraits, arranging your dress so it lies just right, and lighting you in all the right ways.

■ **Benefits:** Such a style means you'll have all the shots you know you want—this person with that person, a formal portrait of you and your new husband that you can put a fancy frame around and hang above the mantel. You could even give your photographer a shot list to make sure he covers everything you want covered.

■ **Drawbacks:** Sometimes the flow of the wedding will be determined by your photographer's need to take a certain picture. You may not want the photographer to have that much control over your event.

Photojournalistic

These days, many photographers will offer photojournalistic services—and they'll also probably tell you right off the bat that they're an *esteemed* photojournalist, as this style has become de rigueur of late. Photojournalism basically means that, by being an observant shutterbug-on-the-wall, your

(Fig. A)
TRADITIONAL PHOTOGRAPHY

MAKE IT PICTURE PERFECT: Be sure to discuss in advance with you

(fig. B)
PHOTOJOURNALISTIC SHOTS

photographer the type of pictures you want shot for your big day.

photographer will capture the story of your wedding day with a series of unposed, candid, in-the-moment pictures. If you'd like a formal portrait or two, or a shot of your great-grandparents dancing together, they'll get that— but their main goal is to show the day through unplanned images: your mom drying your tears with her tissue before you walk out of the bride's room, and your bridesmaids gasping when you walk out; the look your new husband gives you from across the room; the reactions of your guests when the best man toasts with that heinously embarrassing story.

■ **Benefits:** It's these unguarded moments that will take you back to your big day as you're flipping through your album in the years to come.
■ **Drawbacks:** By trying to cover all the dramatic moments photojournalistically, your photographer may miss out on the keepsake photos of loved ones who tend to be outside the main action (older relatives or your wallflower best friend from childhood).

Questions to Ask Your Photographer

Determining the best photographer for your job begins with an interview, so once you've narrowed your choices to your top two, set up a time when you can meet *in person* either in the photographer's studio or at another location where you can see more of his or her portfolio. You can, of course, conduct a phone interview if need be, but you'll get a much better read on whether or not you "click" if you meet face-to-face. Use the sheets on pages 86–87 and in the appendix (pages 218–19) to record pertinent information. While you're reviewing photos from the weddings they've shot, be sure to cover these basics:

■ Have you ever worked at [venue] before?

■ Do you work exclusively with digital photography or do you use film as well? Do you create a mix of color and black and white shots?

■ Do you do a mix of formal and informal?

■ Would you say you're more traditional or photojournalistic?

■ Do you work from a shot list?

■ About how many frames will you take of the event?

■ How long will it take to receive my proofs and to have photos of the event online?

■ Do you do your own printing or do you use a service?

■ How do you handle low-light situations, when using a flash may not be appropriate (during religious ceremonies, for example)?

■ Will you give me final film or a disk containing *all* the images shot?

■ Do you create the wedding albums or do you use a service? Are they included in your packages? What about albums for the parents?

■ How much of a deposit do I need to put down?

■ How do travel and food expenses work into your costs?

Before you sign on with your photographer, be certain that the following issues have been discussed and agreed to in a written contract:

■ Make sure you are guaranteed, in writing, to have the services of the *particular* photographer you've chosen to take pictures on your wedding day. If he or she is the owner of the photography service, make sure the contract specifies the owner by name.

■ Make sure that the contract states what the provisions are if, in an emergency on your wedding day, that photographer can't make it. The two of you should agree on a backup photographer whom you both feel would give you an equivalent service, and have that person named in the contract as well.

Photographer Cheat Sheet

Use this sheet to help choose your wedding photographer. Once you'

PHOTOGRAPHER

MR. ○   MS. ○

Interview: DATE ☐☐ / ☐☐ / ☐☐

Address (Number and Street) | City

State/Province | Country | Zip/Postal Code

TEL ☐☐☐ – ☐☐☐ – ☐☐☐☐

○ HOME   ○ WORK
○ CELL   ○ FAX

Web site | E-mail

Hours | Number of Shots | Price $ ☐☐☐☐☐

SECOND PHOTOGRAPHER

MR. ○   MS. ○

TEL ☐☐☐ – ☐☐☐ – ☐☐☐☐

○ HOME   ○ WORK
○ CELL   ○ FAX

E-mail | Price $ ☐☐☐☐☐

ade your choice, keep his or her contact information close to hand at all times.

PRIME DIRECTIVES

1. Scout venue beforehand to find perfect settings
2. Record and document precious moments and festivities
3. Create a keepsake photo album

■ If you want an extra shooter or two, in addition to your primary photographer, make sure that is specified in the contract—as well as the cost agreed upon by you and your photographer for this extra coverage. Having these extra shooters means that many more moments are captured in photos, and it's often an appealing option for brides whose budgets can accommodate it.

■ Make sure you have a complete understanding of what your photographer's fee entails as far as service, proofs, prints, albums, etc. Don't assume that a flat-fee soup-to-nuts package covers everything from your wedding day till the day you're holding your finished album. You may find the fee buys you their service and proofs only, and that any type of album is extra.

■ Make sure you have an agreement regarding who gets possession and *ownership* of the proofs. Most photographers will give you a stack of 1,100 or so proofs to choose from to create prints for your album, but if you retain the right to all the photos shot, you can always make copies of additional photos further down the road. You may also simply enjoy having "outtakes" that were not quite album-worthy but still convey something of your wedding day.

EXPERT TIP: Don't worry: Most professional photographers have their own boilerplate contract that specifies many of these issues—even the breaks the photographer takes and whether you're expected to feed him or her during the event! You will not have to draw up a document from scratch.

The Videographer

These days, it's likely that your photographer and his assistants won't be the only ones capturing your wedding on film. And unless your cousin Bob's shaky home video is good enough for you when it comes to having audio and visual evidence of the biggest day of your life, you might want to book the services of a professional videographer.

Start by asking your friends who have used videographers, and pay special attention to any people your photographer might recommend. Most important, determine in advance just what kind of video record you want:

- **Documentary?** You'll have a video that records the entire day from start to finish.
- **Interactive?** You'll have plenty of those "say hi to the couple" moments that will make you either cringe or cry.
- **Multimedia?** Your videographer will edit together photos, music clips, and wedding-day footage to create a media montage of you and your spouse's lives before and including your big day.

Shop around for the vendor who best matches your style and budget: Look at examples of the videographer's work, interview the vendor as well as people who've used the services, and sign up him or her with an official contract specifying the services performed on the big day.

The Florist

The florist creates the bouquet that will make you tear up years from now when it's dried and hanging in a shadow box on your wall. But your florist is also the person most responsible for making your wedding décor fabulous and taking your guests' breath away the second they walk into the room. Your florist will help choose the flowers that will drive your décor, setting the tone for your reception and grabbing your guests' attention: It's what they'll see first, and what they'll remember when they recall the magical day or evening they spent with you.

Quick note: This is one of the girlier tasks you'll tackle, so just tell your honey to sit tight while you debate the advantages and disadvantages of going with periwinkle or violet hydrangeas.

Selecting a Florist

There's no way around it: To choose a florist, you must look at photos. Look at bajillions of them—good florists are able to tailor their style to each of their brides, and each of their bride's weddings (venue, style, season, etc.), so looking at one or two of their wedding photos won't give you a complete sense of their abilities.

As you review florist portfolios, keep in mind the criteria that are most important to you and your event:

[1] If, in wedding after wedding, it seems they use a lot of green filler in their arrangements or they seem to favor those ginormous centerpieces that are at least twice the height of your tallest guest, and neither of those is really your thing, they're probably not for you.

FLORIST SELECTION: Talk to your florist about different types of arrangements.

CONTEMPORARY
AND SPARE

CLASSIC
AND OVERSIZED

FRUITS AND
VEGETABLES

PEACOCK
FEATHERS

[2] If you notice certain things about their style that speak to you—they always seem to wrap their brides' bouquets in the prettiest satin ribbon, their arrangements seem impossibly lush and perfectly harmonized with the venue—then pick up the phone and have a chat with them.

[3] Talk to them about your venue, the size of your wedding, and the time of year it will be held to determine whether they have the right level of expertise for your event.

[4] Above all else, be prepared: The flower bill is where a lot of people experience the ultimate sticker shock if they do not prepare a careful budget. You might get one estimate from a florist at the outset, but if you load on expensive blooms and have flowers everywhere throughout your wedding day, that bill is going to quickly add up.

Before you sign a contract with your florist, there are several essential points you should clarify:

■ Make sure you are guaranteed that the owner or whomever you've been working with will be the person setting up your flowers the morning of your wedding. Ask them to detail their Plan B if they can't make it for unforeseen reasons, and make sure Plan B is laid out in the contract as well.

■ Don't be afraid to ask your florist to lay out specifically in your contract what *each* main arrangement will look like (including naming the flower varieties in each arrangement). That way, if you expect an all-white calla lily bouquet and your florist decides the morning of your wedding that green orchids and red hypericum berries would be much lovelier, you can go back to your contract and show her what was agreed upon for the fee. You always want to have things in writing—especially when they're not executed as planned.

■ Verify that your contract specifies a second choice in case a certain bloom falls through and isn't available at the last minute. (Many times your florist will have an idea of what bloom may cause trouble.)

■ Require that your florist coordinates with vendors whose services need to synchronize with the floral arrangements: Is your florist arranging the fresh flowers between the tiers of your wedding cake so that its decoration ties in seamlessly with the rest of the event's flowers? Make sure your florist and baker are buddies (or at least have each other's phone numbers) and know when said arranging is happening. Are you having a nighttime celebration in a grand ballroom—a grand ballroom that's holding an afternoon wedding the same day as yours? Ensure that your florist and the point person at your venue know the second your florist can get in there and start spreading the foliage. Nothing can hold up a wedding like uncoordinated schedules, so check that everyone is on the same page before that morning rolls around.

Determining Your Palette and Flower Choices

Do you remember how, in your pre-engagement days, you'd hear brides-to-be talking about their "colors," or how since you've been engaged everyone's been asking what yours are? The elusive answer mostly lies in the flowers you choose to adorn your wedding day, which will likely determine or be determined by the bridesmaid dresses you choose.

Perhaps you know what colors you want your blooms to be (and from that, the linens and various elements of your décor) the second you know what month your wedding will be. But if you don't, start talking to your florist about where to begin. The season of your wedding is a good a place to start.

- **Fall** lends itself to bold, beautiful hues of wine and burnt orange, gold, green, and chocolate brown.
- **Winter** is a good time for deep jewel tones, like reds, or you could go for a glistening, all-white winter wonderland.
- **Spring** asks for brights and pastels, or a cool palette of all white.
- **Summer** is another good time for bright colors, or a soft beachy palette of light blues, creams, and yellows.

Your florist can steer you toward season-appropriate colors and blooms (don't forget about flower availability), then help you narrow your choices to the colors you'll always think of as your wedding colors long after your wedding photographs have faded.

Unfortunately, flowering your wedding isn't as clear-cut as scratch-and-sniff. And even if you've had an exact vision of what you'd like your flowers to look like at your wedding since forever, the specific circumstances surrounding your real-life wedding could require you to make some adjustments.

For the Season

Some flowers are easily available year-round; others are not. If you're on a strict budget, you'll save yourself a lot of stress by choosing blooms that don't have to be flown in from a remote location where they grow naturally. If you have your heart set on a certain bloom that's tricky to get your hands on during your wedding month and money's no object, you can probably still get your flower by paying a premium—just note that, in some cases, getting flowers that aren't in season could *triple* your costs. Not only that, but blooms unaccustomed to the weather of your wedding day might not hold up before the celebration is over, and you don't want flowers that wear out before you do. Wilted hydrangeas are just sad.

For Your Venue

While there aren't any hard-and-fast rules you must stick to when it comes to selecting the flowers for your reception, a few things are worth thinking about.

■ If you're having a formal, elegant, nighttime, grand-ballroom type of event, gerbera daisies and sunflowers might look a little out of place.

■ Likewise, if your wedding celebration is going to be a beautiful picnic on the grounds of your parents' house, tight arrangements of orchids and deep red roses might look fancier than the rest of the event.

■ Blooms like roses, calla lilies, and other structural flowers look especially nice at nighttime celebrations, which tend to be more formal, whereas flowers such as peonies, hydrangeas, and dahlias look lovely during the day.

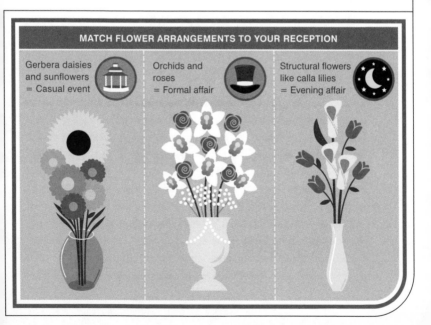

MATCH FLOWER ARRANGEMENTS TO YOUR RECEPTION

Gerbera daisies and sunflowers = Casual event

Orchids and roses = Formal affair

Structural flowers like calla lilies = Evening affair

An experienced florist will probably have handled a wedding at your venue, but if not, take them along on your next visit to the site. Your florist can help you select flowers and arrangements that will complement—or transform—the venue into the vision of your dreams.

For Your Budget

Certain blooms are expensive—as in, *really* expensive. If you already have a vision of what you'd like your flowers to be, run it past your florist before you start signing any checks. If you want an expensive flower and you want it *everywhere*, well, your dress might have to go from being custom-made in Italy to that lovely number you saw on the rack. If you're unwilling to make such a sacrifice, talk to your florist about other possibilities. Lots of flowers look very similar—except for their price tags. A good florist will help you find such alter egos, or they'll help you design arrangements that use your favorite expensive bloom in a way that requires fewer of them.

Determining Your Look

In the past, most pictures of weddings you'd see would have huge, towering, cascading arrangements of who knows what on each tabletop. These were designed so that you could have substantial flower arrangements while still allowing your guests to see one another across the table, resulting in freer conversation and more frequent toasting. (And truly, there is a certain height that blocks that sort of dynamic.) If you love this traditional look, talk to your florist about what you can do to add a little twist, such as submerging blooms in water to fill the empty space between the stems. If these larger-than-life centerpieces aren't exactly your style, there are alternatives that will still make for a meet-and-greet friendly atmosphere at your tables. Multiple low arrangements with a monochromatic color scheme or arranging one bloom per vase will look clean and elegant.

Once you've chosen stephanotis here and orchids there, you can also work with your florist to add some non-floral touches to your centerpiece arrangements—as well as your own bouquet.

■ **Non-Green Elements.** If you want something a little different from a run-of-the mill centerpiece, talk to your florist about accenting yours with elements you don't always see in typical wedding arrangements. You'll be surprised by how creative they can be. Feathers (peacock can be especially striking), branches (willow can look very clean and organic), berries, ribbons, moss, submergible lights, and smooth stones are all additions worth looking into if flowers in clear glass vases aren't exactly getting you excited. Fruits and vegetables such as artichokes, plums, green apples, and kale make gorgeous floral accompaniments and help keep costs down, too.

■ **Family Heirlooms.** Many florists will wrap your bouquet in some sort of lovely satin ribbon (save the hem from your pre-altered dress or use a hem from one of your bridesmaid's dresses to be extra coordinated), but if there's anything special you'd like to have worked into your bouquet, talk to your florist ahead of time. Almost any type of heirloom jewelry can be woven or pinned among the blooms (vintage crystal brooches look especially nice), and old lace handkerchiefs make a lovely alternative to that satin ribbon. Whatever you've got, bring it to one of your meetings with your vendor; your florist can make sure you've got it close by as you walk down the aisle.

A Glossary of Blooms and Bouquets

Florists, much like doctors, may forget from time to time that you are not, in fact, a florist. They toss out the names of different blooms and arrangements, leaving you to ask them to please rephrase their spiel in plain English. Hopefully you can identify a rose by now (and maybe even a few varieties, such as tea and spray?), but for those other, peskier terms, here's a glossary of the more popular blooms to put you a step ahead of the average bride and help you intelligently chat with your florist.

Calla Lily

This structural flower is almost tubular, with a wide, open mouth. It comes in both long and mini versions and is available in a myriad of colors, including ivory, green, pink, yellow, orange, and purples ranging from lilac to dark eggplant. It's available year-round and is fairly expensive. (Note: There are about a million different types of lilies—Asiatic, Stargazer, Oriental, Gloriosa, to name a few—and if you like one, you may like another.)

Hydrangea

This bloom is like a big pouf—just a few stems go a long way. Its petal-filled, bushlike blossom comes in a variety of purples, blues, pinks, and whites and has no scent. Most readily available from July to November and moderately expensive.

Orchid ❁ ❁ ❁ ❁

There are several types of orchids—the cymbidium, dendrobium, phaleanopsis, and mokara being the most widely used for weddings. Collectively, they come in almost any color you'd like and are so striking, just a few can go a long way. Some types can be quite expensive, and most are available year-round.

Peony ❁ ❁

This is a lush, full bloom with a lovely scent. If you are to be a summer bride, chances are you already know you want peonies. In full bloom, they'll be larger than your fist, and they come in colors ranging from white and pale pink to peach to deep magenta. The perfectly round, green buds are also used in arrangements by creative florists. Available from late spring to early summer (though they can be imported during other seasons), they're also one of the most expensive blooms.

Sweet Pea ❁ ❁ ❁

This fairly expensive bloom is available mostly between November and May and is a very popular wedding choice because it looks and smells, well, sweet. The delicate, ruffled blooms come in a variety of colors, from white and apricot to pink, magenta, red, and shades of purple.

Stephanotis ✳✳✳✳

If you're picturing a bride's all-white, perfectly round bouquet, chances are, it's made of stephanotis. With their darling, tiny, star shape; their meaning ("marital happiness"); and their dainty prettiness when dotted with a pearl-headed pin in their center, they are a common choice for brides. The flowers are pure white and available year-round, but, because they grow on a vine, each stem must be individually wired, making them labor intensive and, therefore, expensive.

Dahlia ✳✳

Dahlias are good-sized blooms with an extremely bold shape—round, with layers of slightly pointed petals—that come in a variety of bold colors (pinks, oranges, yellow, reds, and purples). Available from summer through early fall and rather inexpensive, they provide a great bang for your buck.

Anemone ✳✳✳

These vibrant blooms almost look like the love child of a peony and a wide-open tulip—with maybe a little gerbera daisy thrown in. Another November to May flower, they have no scent, are rather expensive, and come in bold hues of pinks, purples, reds, burgundies, and white.

Tulip ❁ ❁ ❁ ❁

Surely you know of the tulip—but perhaps not of the multiple types and color variations that allow for a seemingly endless array of floral arrangements for your wedding. The main varieties are Dutch (the most common), French (longer, slightly more tapered—and expensive), and Parrot (with ruffled petals and striped color combos). Speak to your floral vendor about prices and availability.

Snapdragon ❁ ❁

These blooms grow in tightly packed flowering tubes on long stems in colors ranging from white and pink to bronze, yellow, and arrays of red and purple. They're available mostly in early summer to early fall.

Bonus terms: When deciding the design of your bridal bouquet, keep the following definitions in mind:

Cascade: This shape is the most traditional for a bride's bouquet—one in which the blooms cascade over her hands, as far down as she and her florist like. It creates a very dramatic and rather formal look and is almost always done in all white.

Round: This is the other most common form of bridal bouquet, in which the flowers are loosely arranged and their stems wrapped together. It's a good option for a formal wedding when you don't want the look of the cascade.

Hand-Tied: This casual bouquet has flowers loosely tied, as if you were gathering wildflowers into a bunch in your hand. It's great for less formal, and especially outdoor, weddings.

Nosegay: This bouquet is usually smaller than a typical round bouquet, though it has a similar shape with tightly packed blooms—often, all the same blooms, though you can create one using a variety.

Posy: This is the teeniest version of a bouquet. It features tightly packed small blooms or just a few larger-headed blooms, such as peonies, to make a sweet and simple impact.

Pomander: This shape is often used for your darling flower girl—a ball, hanging from beautiful colored ribbon, usually by the wrist. Popular for this design are roses and hydrangea blooms—anything that looks light and fluffy.

Flower Coordination

Once you've detailed the shape, size, design, and blooms in your own bouquet and centerpieces, don't put away the flower books just yet. Oh, no. Your honey will need a boutonniere. Oh, and so will your dad, your groom's dad, and all the groomsmen. Your bridesmaids need bouquets, too. Your mothers will need some sort of corsage, so that if their fawning and crying and beaming aren't enough, all the world will know that they are The Mothers. Your flower girls and little ring bearers need bloomage, too. And once you've outfitted your people and settled on centerpieces, there are other areas you'll probably want to flower:

■ The place-card table
■ The restrooms (both ladies and gentlemen deserve to look at pretty flowers while they scrub the red wine out of their dress clothes)
■ The gift/card table
■ The favor table
■ And any other area where you'd like to splash your colors (the bar, food stations, etc.)

Don't panic. Your florist knows how to do this. If you don't feel like sweating over these arrangements the way you selected each stem for your own bouquet, just tell him/her what colors/blooms you'd like to focus on, how nuts to go or how limited to be, and let them run with it. They know how to select the right blooms that will pull everything together—and then all the oohing and ahhing will be directed at you.

Chapter 6

Casting Your Reception

Now that you have selected the vendors who will be your "shock troops" on the ground for the entire wedding, it's time to fill in the all-important details of the wedding reception. This is your opportunity to imagine all the purely enjoyable aspects of the day as you gear up to show your guests a truly memorable party with good food, fabulous cake, and music to get everyone out on the dance floor.

The Caterer

Your caterer is responsible for cooking, presenting, and serving the food your guests will eat—and talk about and remember well after your wedding day (especially if it's really good or really bad). Food and drink help set the overall tone of a wedding celebration, so you don't want to just pick any old dude with a chef's hat and a fleet of cater-waiters behind him.

Selecting a Caterer

Happily, because you'll reach this step well after you've finalized your venue, some of the narrowing down of the catering choices will most likely have been done for you. You'll probably find that your venue has either an in-house caterer, which basically means you have to use them (something you should have been well aware of before you signed on with said venue), or a good list of "preferred" caterers, which will include area caterers they've worked with and who will be familiar with the space and function of your venue.

Obviously, if there's one caterer you must use, you can cross that task off your list immediately. But if you have a list to choose from, or

if there are no limitations on who can cater your wedding and you've got to start from scratch, you know the drill:

[1] Consult local wedding magazines and the Web and follow up on word-of-mouth catering recommendations (especially from newlywed friends).

[2] Talk to your wedding planner, venue coordinator, and other vendors about caterers they know, like, and trust.

[3] Investigate the recommended caterers' Web sites to see what kind of food they're best at and what kinds of affairs they frequently cater.

[4] Make a quick phone call to talk to the catering managers and determine whether they're worth further consideration.

[5] Ask about their pricing, service packages, and other business details. Whether you go with a buffet, stations, or a seated dinner, your catering costs will likely come out to be a per-head price—perhaps with a few added costs thrown in (e.g., booze). You'll want to discuss how this all works with the potential caterer before committing.

[6] Once you've narrowed your choices to two or three, get ready to eat. Yes, it's that simple, because now all you really need to know is whether or not you like the caterer's food. A lovely tasting for you and your groom, and perhaps a set of parents, will make or break their candidacy.

⚠ *EXPERT TIP: If it's a toss-up between who makes the best hors d'oeuvres and who makes the best entrée, go with the best dinner selection.*

You can always play up the bar to keep guests happy during the reception-preceding cocktail hour.

Before you sign with your caterer, some essential points will need to be mutually clear:

■ Who will be your point person that day? Ideally, this will be the staffer you've been working with, which is often not the person actually cooking the meals but the catering manager who's leading you through it all. This person should be present on your wedding day to coordinate, execute, and troubleshoot.

■ Make sure your catering contract is to-the-letter specific, for this is most likely the area of your wedding that will have the highest cost attached to it. Specify dates, times, locations, numbers of waitstaff, your exact menu, any allowable substitutions, names, cancellation policies, proof of up-to-date catering licenses, your alcohol agreement (including brands), the timing of service for setting up, preparing, and then serving the various parts of the meal, and of course, what everything costs.

■ Is your caterer providing all the tables, chairs, linens, tableware, serving pieces, and so forth? Or just some of those items? Your florist may be providing some of these, so make sure you know precisely what you need the caterer to supply, then include all those specific and itemized details in your contract as well.

■ What's your caterer's policy on tipping? Ah yes, tipping. This food needs to be served and cleared, many times over, by professional and experienced servers. This alcohol will be served by any number of bartenders. They all deserve a gratuity for their hard work, so talk to your caterer about how that's usually handled. Most won't have gratuities for their staff built into the costs; if they don't, arrange for someone (unfortunately for Dad, it's often him) to give one sum to the catering point person during the reception, which they can then distribute evenly among the various servers.

Designing the Menu

Once you've settled on a caterer, you've got a menu to put together. This task may require some negotiating. Many caterers have a set menu, and while it may be extensive—pages of hors d'oeuvres, entrée selections, special drinks and desserts—perhaps you've got a custom-designed dish you'd like to serve at your wedding reception. Maybe you want to re-create that fantastic pasta you were dining on during the Italian vacation when he popped the question; or maybe no one can make a beef Bolognese better than your grandmother, and she's willing to fork over the recipe. (Note: If you've got your heart set on this dish, make sure your caterer is willing to accommodate before you sign on with them.)

Talk to your caterer. If they're willing, you can do a piecemeal menu, going through their offerings almost like a buffet. You'll select a few of their options and design a few of your own. Once you've hashed out a detailed plan of what you'd like served at various points in the reception (including those hors d'oeuvres, various stations, the entrées, any extracurricular desserts besides the cake, etc.), tie that bib on again. Your caterer will prepare a final tasting for you.

Keep in mind that there are several options when it comes to the catered meal presentation:

■ **The seated dinner.** Your guests will enjoy either butlered or stations of hors d'oeuvres, before sitting down to a soup and/or salad course, dinner entrée, and then some dancing before their slices of cake are plated at their

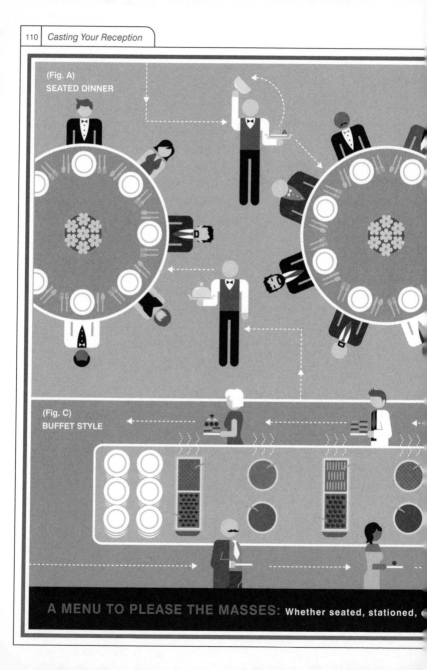

(Fig. A)
SEATED DINNER

(Fig. C)
BUFFET STYLE

A MENU TO PLEASE THE MASSES: Whether seated, stationed,

(Fig. B)
DINNER STATIONS

fet, your reception meal will set the tone for the wedding celebration.

seats. This option is probably the most common, and it allows for guests to sit and relax, drink and toast while being served.

■ **Stations.** After your hors d'oeuvres are passed, guests will take their seats and then visit a series of chef-manned stations. Perhaps you'll have an appetizer station, with salad, a selection of dressings, soups, breads, and spreads. Maybe you'll have a pasta station, where guests can choose a pasta, a sauce, some chicken or shrimp, and a bunch of veggies and have it tossed before them. Maybe you'll have a filet station, where guests can choose a cut of beef or salmon and a few yummy side dishes. Stations allow for movement and perhaps a livelier atmosphere—plus, guests can tailor their meals to their own dietary preferences.

■ **Buffet.** Yep, buffets work for weddings, too. It's certainly more appropriate to serve a buffet meal in a more casual atmosphere as opposed to a grand ballroom, but if the dishes are fantastic, it's unlikely your guests will mind serving themselves. Just work out an efficient system so they're not standing on an hour-long line.

⚠ *EXPERT TIP: When planning a seated dinner with the option of meat or fish, be sure to offer a vegetarian option. Most likely, you'll have a rough idea of how many people would like a penne with fresh veggies and tomato and basil sauce, but instruct your caterer to have a few extra for those guests whose palates you are not familiar with.*

Devising a Seating Chart

Your vendors will need to know just how to set up the guest tables, and for that you will be designing a seating chart. This process doesn't need to be the nightmare it's sometimes touted to be—but you could run into a few "hmm" situations. Hunker down with at *least* your honey, if not also your mom. Be sure to begin this process at least two weeks before the wedding—do *not* leave it for a fun post-rehearsal dinner activity. (You will have bags under your eyes on your wedding day.) It's helpful to have visual aids for this process, whether it's your favorite computer spreadsheet or a bulletin board with sticky notes. Just be sure to use a system that lets you be flexible as you move guests from one table to the next.

Here are the basic decisions you have to make, and the folks they'll involve:

■ **You and your new husband.** Talk with your fiancé about whether you'd like a sweetheart table—which is a table for just you two. You won't be sitting down much during the reception, what with being the center of attention and all, so maybe you'll want a small, separate table that doesn't leave a big gap at your wedding party's table. You can use this table to chill out for a second and spend a few moments with your new spouse. Or perhaps you'd rather hang with your friends at the large wedding party table. After all, you'll have lots of alone time on the honeymoon.

■ **Your wedding party.** Decide whether you want a head table. This can be a long, straight table, or, especially if you have a tiny bridal party, you could sit at a round table with them. Usually, if couples have a sweetheart table, their bridal party will then be scattered among the lay guests' tables, intermixed with their own friends and family. If you don't do a sweetheart table

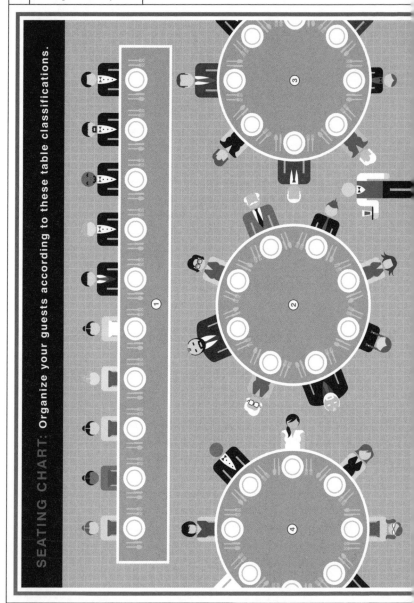

SEATING CHART: Organize your guests according to these table classifications.

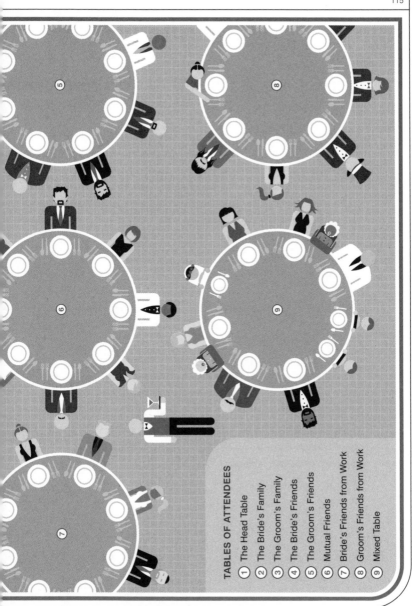

TABLES OF ATTENDEES

1. The Head Table
2. The Bride's Family
3. The Groom's Family
4. The Bride's Friends
5. The Groom's Friends
6. Mutual Friends
7. Bride's Friends from Work
8. Groom's Friends from Work
9. Mixed Table

or a head table, couples often sit with both sets of parents, siblings and their guests, and the officiant and their spouse, if they attend the reception.

■ **Your guests.** This is where some questions can come into play. A lot of it will be easy. You'll group whole tables of friends or family; tables where half of the people know each other and the other half know each other; and some tables that are mixed and matched. Just try to categorize people before you start assigning, and it'll be much easier: your friends and family; his friends and family; people from work; people who know each other; people who don't have a date, etc.

Be aware: You'll need to take special care seating *people who don't get along*. Whether you're talking about divorced parents or your sister and that guy who broke her heart in sixth grade (and she's still not over it), be smart about where you seat them. Alcohol will be flowing freely, so take care not to let confrontations (or even just unnecessary tension) occur by seating them close to one another.

Another special group to consider is your single friends. They'll probably shoot you daggers if you plop them at a table of ten single people, where they all have to sit around staring at each other. Seat them with people they already know, and *then* perhaps a few of your or your groom's single friends they don't know, and you could end up getting all the credit at *their* wedding.

Hashing Out the Booze

This is an area you'll have to work out in precise detail, as it's the area most likely to skyrocket your costs—or, without careful planning, leave you with thirsty guests. Both are equally extremely unpleasant wedding-day scenarios. To make sure neither happens, outline one of these game plans with your caterer beforehand.

■ **Dry Reception.** If you, your fiancé, and any number of your combined families and friends do not drink, and especially if you are contending with a limited budget, feel free to skip the alcohol altogether. Serve lots of fun non-alcoholic drinks, including sparkling juices, and everyone can toast to your happiness just the same.

■ **A Limited (or Pre-Chosen) Bar.** This option basically means the alcohol will flow freely at your reception—but with you in control of what is served and when. This is probably the most widely employed option for a wedding reception, because it's really not restrictive but does allow you some options for containing costs. Let's say you'll serve both red and white wines and Champagne for the toast, have a selection of bottled beers, and offer any mixed drinks that can be made with sodas, juices, vodka, and rum (you pick the brands). Then, you can instruct your caterer to keep the bar open during the cocktail hour(s) and dessert hour(s). During the reception, when guests are seated and either listening to toasts or eating, make sure waiters are constantly circling, equipped with wine and perhaps beer. Either or both of these options will make a significant dent in your alcohol costs, without leaving anyone wondering where their next drink is coming from.

■ **An Open Bar.** This option is for those couples who (a) have no budgetary limits and/or (b) have no worries about any particular friend or uncle

getting bombed and making a scene. An open bar means just that—it's open all the time, as are your guests' options for what to drink. You can still pick the brands of alcohol that will be served, but there are no other limits. It's a very gracious option for your guests but perhaps not for the financiers of your wedding, who will indeed be charged for each and every guzzled sip. And truly, it does heighten the risk for those already prone to imbibing heavily to get out of control and make an embarrassing speech/break their ankle and possibly someone else's on the dance floor/puke all over the ice sculpture. If you're going with the open bar, assign a trustworthy buddy to each suspect to keep an eye on them should they start double-fisting.

■ **A Cash Bar.** Just don't do it. You might as well charge a cover to get into your reception and have a 6'5", 300-pound bouncer named Bubba standing at the door and asking your guests if they're on the list.

⚠ *EXPERT TIP: Ask your caterer and/or venue about the possibility of your buying your own alcohol and delivering it the day before the ceremony. This may translate into a substantial cost savings.*

The Baker

Your baker is responsible for creating the main focus of those standard-issue wedding photos: the cake. If the cake is spectacular, people will be impressed and remember it; if it's awful, people will ignore it in lieu of dancing and more drinks—*and* remember it. If you follow wedding traditions, the cake also provides the opportunity to relive part of your wedding day later on, as you hack into that top tier on your first anniversary.

Selecting a Baker

This decision may be even more limited than your catering selections since your caterer may be accustomed to providing wedding cakes as well. You can check out your caterer's cake work (i.e., eat ten slices) and see if you want one included in your package. But if your caterer doesn't specialize in cakes, gather some baker options the same way you've gathered information on all your other potential vendors (via word of mouth, magazines, Web sites, recommendations from other vendors), and start making calls.

If you like the baker after talking to him or her on the phone, and like what you've seen of their style, go ahead and check them out in person. It should be easy to convince your honey to come along for this trip; it will consist of nothing but eating cake.

Selecting the Cake

Once you've settled on a baker, it's time for the fun work of selecting the details. Chances are, when you decided on a certain baker, it was after tasting some fabulous confection—and perhaps you already know the cake that sealed the deal (e.g., their red velvet with chocolate mousse filling and buttercream icing or their butter pound with Grand Marnier–soaked raspberry-preserves filling and chocolate fondant icing).

If you were sold on the baker but not necessarily one of their premade cakes, however, head back over to the bakery:

■ Take along your ideas—pages ripped out of tons of magazines, notes from your florist, anything printed off the Web, the things you've pictured in your head—and say you're open to all flavors.
■ Sometimes the baker will set out slices of various combinations of cake, filling, and frosting. Other times, they'll set out each component separately, allowing you to try various combinations of the three parts of the cake to find what you like best.
■ If you have a recipe you want them to try (Grandma's famous chocolate chip pound cake), make sure you ask upfront if they're willing to give it a whirl.

This decision-making process should be a fun one; after all, you're basically slapping together different forms of sugar, so how can you go wrong?

Before you sign with your baker, there are several essential points to clarify:

■ If you want sketches of your cake included in your contract, outlined with flavors and decorations and colors and sizes, ask for that.
■ Make sure that all costs are clearly outlined in the contract. Most bakers will charge you a per-person price (meaning, once you have your final head

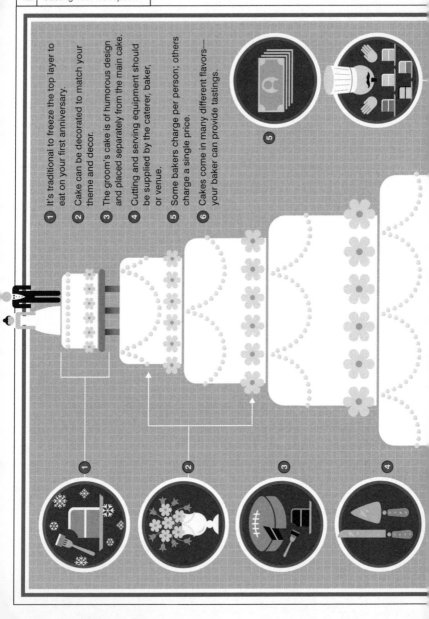

1. It's traditional to freeze the top layer to eat on your first anniversary.

2. Cake can be decorated to match your theme and decor.

3. The groom's cake is of humorous design and placed separately from the main cake.

4. Cutting and serving equipment should be supplied by the caterer, baker, or venue.

5. Some bakers charge per person; others charge a single price.

6. Cakes come in many different flavors—your baker can provide tastings.

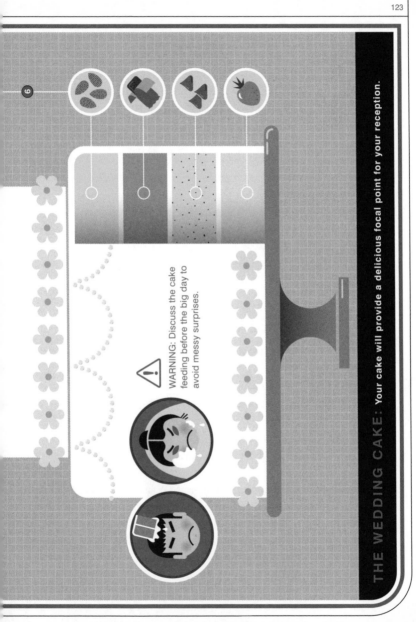

WARNING: Discuss the cake feeding before the big day to avoid messy surprises.

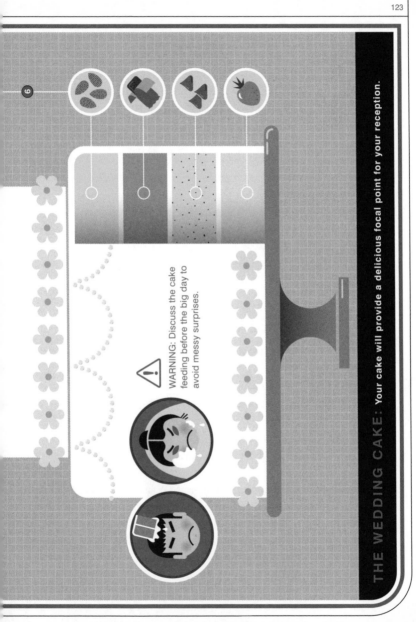

THE WEDDING CAKE: Your cake will provide a delicious focal point for your reception.

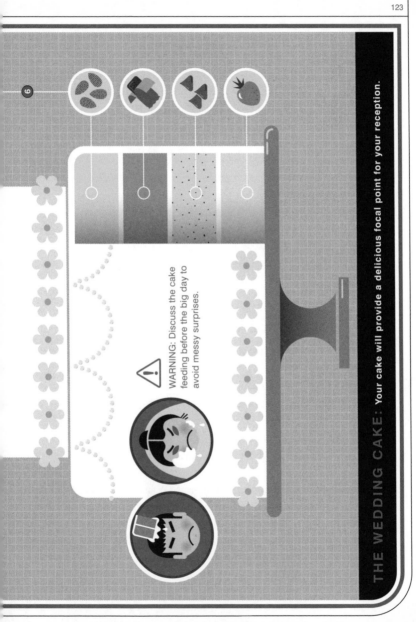

count, they'll make the cake as big as it needs to be and charge you accordingly), but others may have just one charge.

■ Make sure the baker is clear where the cake will be placed (both the address of your venue and the exact area inside the reception room where you want it), and the time they should arrive to set it up.

■ Make sure they're coordinating with other vendors involved in setting up the wedding cake: the florist, to add some fresh-flower touches; the caterer, if they're adding other plates of desserts to the same table (especially something like a chocolate fountain).

■ Be clear about whether you're renting cake-cutting and cake-serving equipment from them; if not, your caterer or venue will need to provide these items.

A Glossary of Icing Terms

There's a lot more out there than those cans of Duncan Hines you dive into when you get into a fight with your fiancé. Here are a few of the most commonly used icing terms, so you can work with your baker to choose the ones you want adorning your lovely cake.

■ **Buttercream:** The most basic icing we all know and love. Made mainly from butter and sugar, it can go on top of the cake as a covering or between the layers as a filling.

■ **Fondant:** Have you noticed how most wedding cakes look impossibly smooth? That's because they've been covered in fondant, a sugar- and water-based, super thick, malleable icing that can be rolled out like dough.

■ **Marzipan:** If you've seen a cake with pretty, perfectly formed fruits or other decorations, they're probably made from this paste of sugar and ground bitter almonds.

■ **Gum paste/Pastillage:** This basically dry but malleable sugar dough makes cake decorations that are long-lasting and edible (though only *technically*, if you know what we mean).

■ **Ganache:** A thick, chocolate-y glaze poured atop fancy desserts, creating a surface so shiny you can check your makeup in it.

■ **Spun sugar:** Basically fancy-pants cotton candy; it is "flossier" looking, almost like long, super-thin strands of colored glass, and often used for a delicate touch around tiers of the cake.

To Be Messy or Not to Be Messy?

Ah, this is a big one. Throughout all your wedding planning, perhaps no question will plague you as much as the one about whether your wedding cake will be a thing of beauty or food-fight fodder. It's a toughie—and you and your fiancé might not really be able to answer it for yourselves until you're in the heat of the moment. The question basically comes down to this: Is it more important

(a) that this moment exemplify the fun relationship you have with each other, and the humor between the two of you (recorded with the lightheartedness and excellent photo ops that could go along with this moment), or

(b) that your hair, makeup, and dress stay intact and frosting-free for the remainder of the evening?

If you want to make absolutely sure you're both on the same page, you had better discuss this issue before the Big Day. If your darling hub-to-be is the type you think could agree to keep you squeaky clean but then turn around and shove buttercream up your nose come your wedding day, you've either got to be prepared for the worst or make sure he understands that he won't enjoy his wedding night nearly as much if he pulls this kind of stunt. This is one moment of your wedding day that can't be spelled out in Excel.

The Groom's Cake

Remember the scene in *Steel Magnolias* where Shirley MacLaine hacks off the rear end of a gray armadillo and plops it onto Tom Skerritt's plate, revealing its deep, blood-red insides? That's a groom's cake. It's usually a whimsical or humorous design, placed separately from the main confection, and you can either serve it along with the other cake at the reception or box it up for your guests to take home. If you've got a creative idea for a cake, one that reflects your interests, hobbies, or likes as a couple, but you don't want to mess with tradition, a groom's cake might be the way to go. Plus, if your groom is challenging you on many an idea you don't want to budge on for the main cake, offer him his own cake, and let him do whatever he wants with it. (After all, it's probably one of the few wedding preparation decisions he'll get to make.)

The Music

When it comes to the flow and vibe of your party, music is the number one item that will set it, move it, and keep it going. It's also another area fraught with decision, beginning with the main one: Who shall be the emcee of your party—a DJ with a headset and a booth of spinning records or a bandleader with a microphone and a small army of musicians behind him?

Band vs. DJ

"Band vs. DJ" is one of the oldest debates in the wedding world. What it comes down to, ultimately, is your budget and your preference.

You might as well know this up-front—a band will cost more than a DJ. Sometimes, significantly more. Simply put, there are more people involved with the band option, and more people means more logistics: These people will need to eat and will need a staging/break area; and they can't go on for hours on end, even if it looks like your party might. Some additional pros and cons:

Pros:

■ A band can control the pacing of the party—a good bandleader can be the charismatic emcee of your entire party, reading the crowd, controlling the pacing of the music as well as the tempo of the songs.

■ If the bandleader is funny or the band wears great costumes, it can add something extra to the night.

■ Many wedding bands come with a sound system that should be able to play songs just as a DJ would, if there's a hit you simply have to hear in its original form.

■ There's an energy a live band brings to a party that can't be duplicated by a sound system.

Cons:

■ Even the best wedding/cover band can't play your favorite songs and make them sound exactly like the original.

■ Did I mention that a band is more expensive?

A DJ can also be an excellent emcee of the party, with the same skills as the bandleader for reading a crowd and the party. He'll

SELECTING ENTERTAINMENT FOR THE RECEPTION

**(Fig. A)
BAND**

PROS

1. A band controls pacing of the party
2. Personality of band adds to the festivities
3. Can play recorded songs with sound equipment
3. Bands bring an energy to an event that can't be duplicated

CONS

1. Can't play songs exactly like the recorded version
2. More expensive than a DJ

**(Fig. B)
DJ**

PROS

1. DJs are cheaper than hiring a band
2. All songs sound like the original version
3. DJ keeps music coming easily during breaks
4. DJ can play a variety of bands and styles

CONS

1. DJs have a less personal feel
2. Bad DJs are worse than bad bands

know what to play to keep the vibe calm during dinner or upbeat when you want your guests flooding the dance floor. Some additional pros and cons:

Pros:

■ DJs are cheaper. Hiring one person with a bunch of equipment and feeding just one person can mean the difference of thousands of dollars.

■ Every song you want to hear at your wedding will sound exactly like the original—because it is the original.

■ A simple press of a button ensures that the music continues when the DJ takes breaks.

■ A DJ can generally stretch for more variety in song selection than a band that may specialize in one mode of performance.

Cons:

■ DJs don't lend as personal a feel as a band does. They don't have the same visual impact as a group of musicians decked out in finery and in the swing of the event.

■ Somehow, a bad DJ always seems worse than a bad band. Extra nasty ones will ignore requests and play painful clichés like the Macarena or chicken dance.

In the end, both the band and DJ options have an equal number of pros and cons. You need to decide for yourselves which choice suits you best—and what your budget allows.

Choosing Your Music Maker

Once you've settled on whether it will be a band or a DJ bringing your party into the night, narrow down your choices, and get this process started as early as you can. Although you needn't figure out every last musical detail, the most popular musicians will be booked up to a year in advance, and you don't want to get stuck with a second-rate party.

This time, however, your main method for choosing this vendor will most likely be word of mouth. If a band or DJ is really good, word spreads: any recent newlyweds you know, your venue manager, or any of your other vendors should be able to tell you their top three choices right off the bat. Once you've got a few in the running, go and see them. After all, if you're not into their style or personality, you're not going to want them dictating the course of your reception with the tunes they play. They'll tell you when their next performance is—even if it's some-one else's wedding. You can go along and hang in the back for a few minutes to see if you like what you hear. And don't worry about being a crasher—chances are, there will be a couple or two poking their noses into your reception for the same reason.

Choosing a Playlist

Whether you've hired a band or a DJ, you and your fiancé will want to work up a playlist. This might even be a fun time to invite a few members of your bridal party and get as much input as possible on your wedding soundtrack. When it comes to the open dance floor portion of the night, request a few songs you'd like to hear—and definitely mention those that make you cringe—but otherwise let your band or DJ do their job. When it comes to other parts of the reception, however, go ahead and list away—these are times when *everyone* will be paying attention.

Entrance Songs

Please, don't list the theme song to *Rocky*. Just don't. Your new husband will hardly be able to resist the urge to run in, pumping his fists in the air, and that's probably not the image you have of your first appearance in a room as husband and wife. Instead, pick songs for your entrance and your bridal party's entrances that mean something to you and are upbeat. Was there a song you would have liked to have for your first dance, but it's a little too jazzy for a romantic slow dance? Pick that for the two of you. And there's got to be a song that always reminds you and your girlfriends (and him and his buddies) about some fun time of your life—maybe the song you listened to with your college roommates as you got ready for a night on the town, or one that always makes you laugh because it was the cheesy theme of your high school prom. Go ahead and pick whatever songs make you happy—they'll only be playing for a few short moments anyway.

First Husband/Wife Dance

Don't worry if the two of you don't have a "song." Not everyone will have experienced some profound moment in their relationship while the perfect, smooth, slow song was playing in the background. If you do, of course, go for it—it will solidify the tune as *truly* your song. But if not, pick a song that you love for both its melody and its meaning to you. The lyrics could describe the way you feel about each other or the type of relationship that you two have. It may not even be the song itself that makes it for you— maybe you just knew he was the one at a certain group's concert, and so anything they sing brings back those feelings. Just don't pick your song randomly, or because it's taking too long to figure one out, or because you can't agree. Ask your bandleader or DJ for some suggestions, or ask around. And don't be afraid to do something out of the ordinary: Remember that song Adam Sandler sang to Drew Barrymore on the plane in *The*

1. ENTRANCE SONG

- ❏ "We Go Together" by the cast of *Grease*
- ❏ "Beautiful Day" by U2
- ❏ "Bittersweet Symphony" by the Verve
- ❏ "Love and Marriage" by Frank Sinatra

2. FIRST DANCE

- ❏ "A Moment Like This" by Kelly Clarkson
- ❏ "All I Want Is You" by U2
- ❏ "Come Away with Me" by Norah Jones
- ❏ "Let's Stay Together" by Al Green

3. FATHER/DAUGHTER DANCE

- ❏ "Butterfly Kisses" by Bob Carlisle
- ❏ "Isn't She Lovely" by Stevie Wonder
- ❏ "My Girl" by the Temptations
- ❏ "The Way You Look Tonight" by Frank Sinatra

YOUR WEDDING SOUNDTRACK: Here are a few suggestions for some o

4. CROWD PLEASERS/LAST DANCE

- ❏ "ABC" by the Jackson Five
- ❏ "Dancing Queen" (or anything else) by Abba
- ❏ "Lady Marmalade" by Labelle
- ❏ "Love Shack" by the B-52s
- ❏ "Papa's Got a Brand New Bag" by James Brown
- ❏ "Play That Funky Music" by Wild Cherry
- ❏ "Respect" by Aretha Franklin
- ❏ "Shout" by Otis Day and the Nights
- ❏ "Sweet Caroline" by Neil Diamond
- ❏ "Twist and Shout" by the Isley Brothers or the Beatles
- ❏ "We Are Family" by Sister Sledge
- ❏ "YMCA" by the Village People

re important dances that will take place at your wedding reception.

Wedding Singer? "I Wanna Grow Old with You" is as simple and beautiful a message as any to put on the dance floor during this classic moment.

Father/Daughter Dance

When it comes to this category, there are plenty that seemed written specifically for this purpose; in fact, many male musicians have actually written songs for their daughters. You can choose any of these or even go a little outside the box, opting for songs in which the singer is just singing about a "she" in a nonromantic way. Chances are, while playing through the options, one will hit you as perfect for the specific relationship between you and your father. Your hired musician can be of help, too, offering songs you may not already know. This is also one song that's nice to decide on together with your father—you never know, he may have been thinking about this since you were a little girl. (Dads can pull out all sorts of surprises when their daughters are getting married.)

The Last Dance

Leave "Last Dance" behind at your prom and choose a song that conveys a feeling of joy, whether it's about new beginnings, a solid love, or a really good time being had by all. If you're unsure how you want to end the night, don't be afraid to leave it up to your musicians. This is their job, and if you did your homework before hiring them, they will do it well.

Before signing with your band or DJ, there are several essential points to clarify:

■ If you're hiring a band but would like to hear a song or two in its original form and have coverage during the musicians' breaks, make sure they've got a DJ sound system that can be used for both purposes. If they don't, have an alternate plan to ensure there's never silence on the dance floor. (You may want to employ a willing bridesmaid and/or groomsman with good taste and an iPod.)

■ If using a band, make sure the details are laid out contractually: when they will get there; how long they'll play; what they should wear; if you need to feed them dinner; the names of the band members (most important, the leader and his stand-in in case of an emergency); any songs you want to be sure are played (or not played); any possible overtime fee; how many breaks they'll take; and what each and every last detail costs.

■ If you're hiring a DJ, make sure your contract stipulates that the DJ you hired will actually be there for your event. It should also state the name of an acceptable replacement should an emergency arise.

■ When finalizing the DJ's contract, be sure to indicate what equipment the DJ will bring and what, if anything, you have to provide, such as a table and chair, food, etc. Outline his exact start and end times (plus when he will and won't be playing during the reception), as well as any overtime fees, if you should wish him to stay and bring the party home.

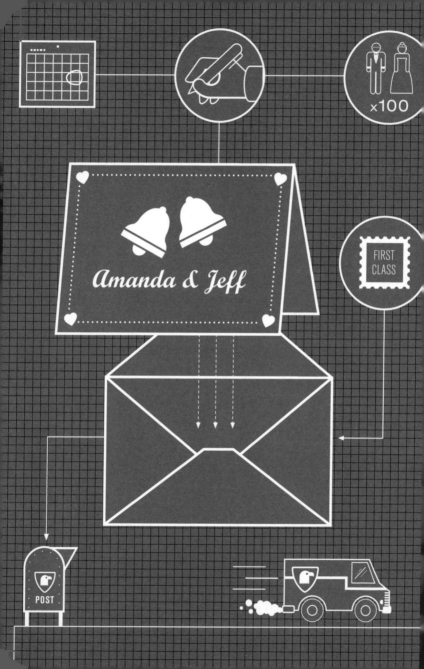

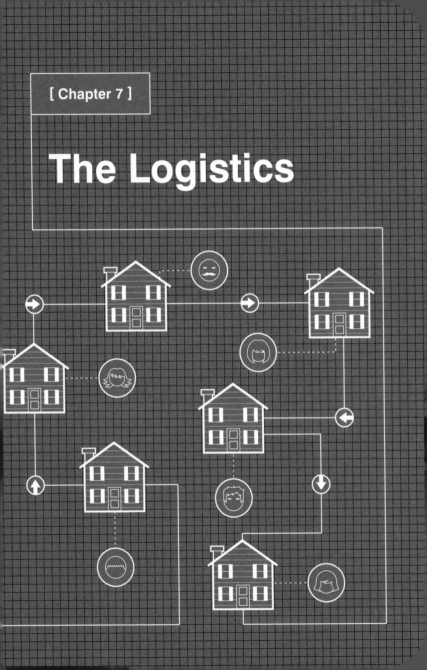

[Chapter 7]

The Logistics

Yes, planning a wedding can feel like a job sometimes. Especially when you reach the pre-wedding tasks that simply *must* be done for your wedding to take place. We're not talking about the niceties of floral arrangements and place cards at the reception, but rather the logistics that will make sure your event functions like a well-oiled machine—and most important, the logistics that will ensure that your guests feel cared for and honored to be at your big event.

Here are some of the biggies.

The Invitations

There's no way around it: Formally inviting guests to your wedding is a must, unless you're doing a just-the-two-of-you-on-the-beach or in-the-judge's-chambers event. You'll want to take some time choosing or designing your invitations to set the tone for your celebration from the moment your guests open their envelopes.

Save-the-Dates and Invite Timing

A "save the date" card is easily purchased at your favorite stationer and does not need to be of the same quality or design as your ultimate invitations. The idea is to make sure all your guests know the date to set aside, so as soon as you have a set-in-stone wedding date, feel free to send 'em out! Even if it's a whole year before, go ahead—just make sure they go out at *least* six months ahead of time.

Of note:

■ Along with your save-the-date, try to include hotel information (more on that later) for out-of-town guests who may need to book travel plans far in advance.

■ Don't worry if it turns out that you didn't send a save-the-date to everyone who ends up on your guest list. Chances are, you've sent them to the most important people on that list, and your event has been penciled in.

■ The invitations that come later will fill in all the details: times, locations, directions, and transportation information.

Invitations should arrive in your guests' mailboxes about eight weeks before your wedding—time enough for guests to confirm that they can come, make travel arrangements if necessary, and get those response cards back to you. (Remember, you'll need to give certain vendors a head count about a week or two before the wedding so they can finalize their planning.) In order to get those invites into mailboxes eight weeks before the big day, you'll have to start researching your options at least five months ahead of time. You'll need sufficient time to design the invites, proof them, and correct any errors before they are printed. Don't back yourself up against a wall with this one, or you'll be scrambling just to get them out in time.

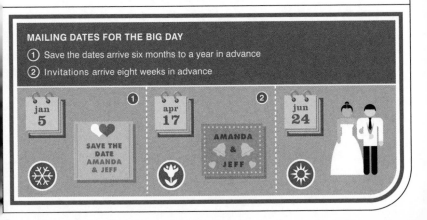

MAILING DATES FOR THE BIG DAY
① Save the dates arrive six months to a year in advance
② Invitations arrive eight weeks in advance

jan 5

SAVE THE DATE AMANDA & JEFF

apr 17

AMANDA & JEFF

jun 24

The good news is that this is an area where you can keep your costs down if you wish—so that your bridesmaids can carry all-peony bouquets or you and your groom can go with platinum bands instead of white gold. Spend some time looking around and comparing prices. Pick as plain and classic a design as possible if you want to stay within a tighter budget. On the other hand, if you're artsy and really want to impress your guests with spectacular invites, there are plenty of options these days for designing them yourself, and lots of talented designers willing to work with you on a custom design that will get your party off on the right foot.

Choosing a Stationer

You'll be relying on not only visuals and samples to get the "look and feel" of your stationery choices, but also the tried-and-true techniques you used to research all your other vendors: Ask around to get word-of-mouth recommendations; research stationers on the Web and in local wedding mags; and flip through wedding invitations you've saved because you knew someday you might like to use a similar design.

When you've narrowed down your list, make an appointment to talk to each designer in person to see how they do things in their shop. Ask

■ Whether they have books of pre-made invites you can page through and choose from;

■ Whether they do only custom-designed invitations or have less expensive standard designs;

■ What is included in the different packages they offer (so you can make sure save-the-dates, menu cards, place cards, programs, and invitations all look coordinated);

■ Whether they carry open stock in various colors, so that you might partly design your own.

Now find out what services they offer; how long the design, proof, and print processes take; and how their pricing works (yep, there's more than one way to put words on a card):

■ **Engraving.** This super-expensive method uses a metal machine to actually press the words of your invite into the paper, and it takes 4–6 weeks.

■ **Thermography.** This is a commonly used and less expensive method, in which a heat process stamps the letters to the paper to form raised lettering. Thermography also takes less time than engraving (3 weeks), but will still work well for formal affairs.

■ **Letterpress.** This is another expensive method—but it allows for a very clean, rich look to the words on the page. You can also play around with colors with this option. Allow at least 4–6 weeks for letterpress invites.

■ **Embossing.** Because this method of creating raised lettering is so expensive, many couples will use embossing for an extra touch only—perhaps around the invitation border. It also looks lovely with large initials. You will need to allow 4 weeks for embossing.

And now, it's time to pick your papers. Ask the stationer about the various papers and inks available (there's a whole world of textures, thicknesses, finishes, colors, and pigments). Some stationers, beyond having glassine, jacquard, marbled, and mylar paper, will also print on glass, wood, or silk—mediums you may have never even imagined.

Choosing Your Design

Your invitations provide your guests' first impression of what your party will be like, so you certainly want them to properly reflect the wedding you've planned. The formality of your invites, the timing of the events, and the setting will tell your guests what sort of attire is expected. Some couples will explicitly spell out black tie, black tie optional, dressy/casual, etc., but don't be surprised if you end up fielding calls from guests asking whether by "black tie" you mean that sports coats are OK.

If you're going to have a grand, formal affair, you might choose thick, ecru stock with classic black script and gold on the inside of the envelope. You'll use traditional wording, saying something like, "Mr. & Mrs. Smith request the honor of your presence as their daughter, Megan, marries Paul on Saturday, the twentieth of October, at half-past two in the afternoon," and so forth.

If you're having a slightly less formal affair, perhaps you'd like to go with a fun color combination, a whimsical design, and looser wording: "Please join Mr. & Mrs. Jones as their daughter, Amy, marries Patrick on Saturday, October 20th, at 2:30 in the afternoon."

There aren't any hard-and-fast wording rules. The only thing to be mindful of is honoring the people hosting your wedding.

If your parents are hosting:
Mr. & Mrs. Brown request the honor of your presence as their daughter, Christa, marries Joe on Saturday, the twentieth of October, at half-past two in the afternoon.

If both sets of parents are hosting:
Mr. & Mrs. Brown, along with (or "and") Mr. & Mrs. Johnson, request the

YOUR WEDDING DAY STATIONERY

Please join Mr. & Mrs. Jones
as their daughter,
Emily
marries
Justin
On Saturday,
October 20th,
at 2:30 in the afternoon

*Mr. & Mrs. Brown request the honor
of your presence as their daughter,
Joan Brown
marries
John Cassidy
On Saturday
the Twentieth of October,
at half-past two in the afternoon*

①

THE FAVOUR OF A REPLY IS
REQUESTED ON OR BEFORE
MAY 14, 2008
Mr. & Mrs. John Heyman
ACCEPT WITH PLEASURE
—— PETITE FILET & SHRIMP WELLINGTON
—— CITRUS CHICKEN
—— VEGETARIAN
—— DECLINE WITH REGRET

②

Amanda
&
Jeff
October 20th, 2008

MENU

Salad

Hot Items

Dessert

③

*The Celebration
of Marriage Uniting
Melissa Stanley
and
Bill Canton*

*Saturday, June 24, 2008
2:00 p.m.
Queen of the Most Holy
Rosary Church
Smalltown, Pennsylvania*

④

MR. ROBERT COLE
TABLE 3

⑤

⑥

ALL PRINTED MATTER

① Invitations
② RSVP card
③ Menu cards
④ Ceremony programs
⑤ Place cards
⑥ Labels for favors

honor of your presence at the marriage of their children, Christa and Joe, on Saturday, the twentieth of October, at half-past two in the afternoon.

If you and your fiancé are hosting:
Christa and Joe request the honor of your presence at their marriage. Or: Please join us as we get married on Saturday, October 5, at 2:30 in the afternoon.

Looking for ways to make your invitations stand out? Talk to your stationer about creating magnets for save-the-dates or including black-and-white photo-booth strips in your invitations. There's really no limit to what a creative person can do—just make sure you find out what it all costs before you slap down that plastic.

If you'd like to coordinate all your designed papers, talk to your stationer about the additional items you'd like them to print:

■ RSVP card, return envelope, directions card, hotel info, and any other components inside the invitation
■ menu cards for each guest's seat
■ ceremony programs
■ place cards
■ labels for favors or other small items (personalized wine and beer labels, for example)

Also discuss whether your stationer provides calligraphy services for addressing the envelopes or if they can recommend a few professionals. (Unless, of course, you have perfect penmanship and plan to address them yourself while watching *American Idol*.)

Transportation

Transportation logistics for your big event may seem like a no-brainer since you rarely give thought to how you get from point A to point B most days of the year—which is probably why it's one of the last things harried brides realize they need to arrange for themselves, their wedding party, and their guests.

The fact is, you're not going to be able to stuff yourself and your layers of tulle behind the wheel of your car and simply chauffeur yourself over to the ceremony—you're going to need some help. Your bridesmaids, your parents, and your dear groom and his groomsmen will all need to get to the wedding site, too. And your guests will probably need some help as well.

This all sounds daunting, but just take each part of the day and plan accordingly. The key here is to communicate the transportation plan to each group beforehand.

For You and Your Peeps

Before tucking into bed the night before your wedding, you will have a plan detailing how you and your bridal party are getting where you need to go. The time frame for transportation should take into account possible traffic jams and other snafus, so calculate the usual time for the trip and then double it just to be safe.

Here are the main trips and cargo your hired drivers will need to transport via Rolls-Royce, limo, trolley, horse and buggy, or what have you.

■ You, your parents, and the bridal party, from wherever you're getting ready to the ceremony site (Fig. A)

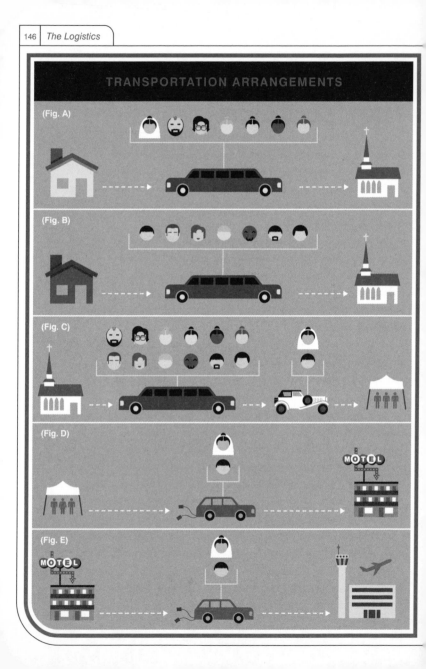

- Your husband-to-be, his parents, and his groomsmen, from wherever they're getting ready to the ceremony site (Fig. B)
- You and your new husband from the ceremony to the reception site (Fig. C)
- Your parents and bridal party from the ceremony to the reception site (Fig. C)
- You and your new husband from the reception to wherever you're staying that night (Fig. D)
- You and your new husband from wherever you stayed on your wedding night back to your home or your parents' home or to the airport for your honeymoon (Fig. E)

For Your Guests

If several guests are staying at a hotel or two near your wedding site, it's a nice idea to provide a shuttle to and from the hotel and both the ceremony and reception sites. Your guests won't have to figure out who's going in what car, bother with directions that might make them, and therefore your party, late, or worry about whether they've had two gin and tonics or twelve. Arrange with the hotel to hire a nice trolley, bus, or van and a helpful, knowledgeable, and sober driver. Alternatively, your wedding planner or the manager at your wedding site may be able to recommend the transportation services of vendors they frequently use at the site.

Here are the main trips you'll arrange for your guests:

- From the hotel to the ceremony
- From the ceremony back to the hotel and then to the reception site, if there's a break before the reception, or from the ceremony to the reception venue
- From the reception back to the hotel where the guests are staying

Taking Care of Your Out-of-Town Guests

For at least a good handful of your guests, receiving your invitation will be a prompt not only to pop your so nicely stamped reply cards back in the mail, but to book expensive flights to your wedding, along with car rentals and hotel rooms. On top of all that, they'll be buying you a lovely wedding present and maybe taking some time off work if they need to catch a certain flight to get to the festivities on time.

Now, because these are people whom you've invited, and who have responded yes to your wedding, we can assume you love them and they love you, and they are, of course, happy to do all this. But it's still quite a lot to ask. The best way to show them how much you appreciate all they did to be there with you on your big day is to treat them graciously during the time they're in town, providing anything that will make their stay both easier to navigate and more fun.

The Things You've Got to Do

For the most part, this entails providing your guests with information, information, information. Your invitations should either include all of this information or refer people to a Web site or other resource where they can find all the logistics in one place:

■ Flight and train options for those arriving from far away (plus any group-discount options you've researched), along with the names of car rental companies at the local airport.

■ Directions for those driving from neighboring vicinities.

■ At least two hotel options (three is even nicer), with different price ranges but all close to the ceremony and wedding locales. (Be sure to negotiate a group discounted rate for a block of rooms for your wedding weekend. The hotel will quote both the price as well as the date by which your guests must book to receive it.)

■ Transportation, as outlined above, to and from all the wedding festivities, since many guests may choose not to rent a car.

■ A schedule of events. It's courteous to invite your out-of-town guests to all pre-wedding festivities, such as the rehearsal dinner. The schedule will help them plan where they have to be and when, so they can arrange their recreation schedule accordingly.

The Things That Are Nice to Do

Now that you've informed your guests about every last thing they need to know directly related to your wedding, and you have provided both transportation and sheltering options, you've technically fulfilled your bridal-hosting duties. But let's be serious. Wouldn't you be a little miffed if you traveled far and shelled out serious coin to attend a wedding, and all you got was a list of events? Free drinks can go only so far.

There are some extra touches you can do for your out-of-town guests to turn their little trip from a wedding weekend into a mini-vacation. Consider some of these options:

The Welcome Basket

Imagine getting off a long flight, stumbling into your hotel room knowing you've got to be cleaned up and ready for a party in an hour, and seeing a basket/bag/bucket filled with goodies at the foot of the bed. That'd make it all a little better, wouldn't it?

Goody baskets are a great way to welcome your guests (since it'd be a little hard to be waiting for each of them in their rooms, party hats and noise makers in hand, upon each and every arrival), and thank them right up-front for coming. You can include:

■ bottled water (maybe personalized with the bride and groom's names)
■ bags of gourmet coffee
■ hangover pills
■ sleep masks filled with cooling gel
■ little snacks
■ packets of info listing all your favorite area shopping, dining, spa-ing (for those lady guests who didn't have time to get a fresh pedi before hopping their flight), and sight-seeing spots, including contact information for each one.

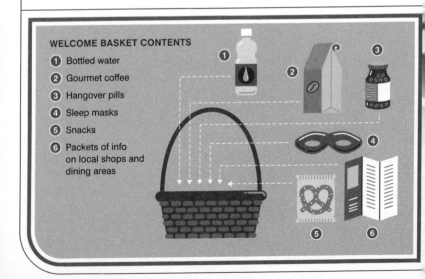

WELCOME BASKET CONTENTS
1 Bottled water
2 Gourmet coffee
3 Hangover pills
4 Sleep masks
5 Snacks
6 Packets of info on local shops and dining areas

Your guests will have free time, after all, and who better than you to suggest where they spend it? Even throw in a few location-specific touches: a couple of super-soft pretzels and Tastykakes if you're in Philadelphia; a coupon for Ghirardelli chocolate if you're in the Bay Area; a couple of bagels from your favorite shop if you're in New York City. These are the things that are really going to wow your guests—and let them know that you're totally pumped they came.

Extra Events

As we said earlier, it's customary these days for out-of-town guests to be invited to the rehearsal dinner—but what if that's Friday night, and many guests are coming in Thursday? (This happens especially when you're hosting a destination wedding on an island, and everyone's coming in to make a little trip of it.) Host a small welcome reception at your favorite restaurant. You don't have to buy everyone dinner, but buying them drinks and offering some passed hors d'oeuvres is a start.

If you are in a tropical setting for a destination wedding, think about arranging a sunset cruise that first night to get everyone acquainted and in a festive mood. You could even plan other outings, depending on how long everyone's around, like group bowling, golfing, or trips to the outlets just outside your city. These activities should be completely optional, of course—this isn't summer camp—but you'll find that guests who are completely unfamiliar with your area and didn't plan a free-time itinerary really appreciate having options laid out for them.

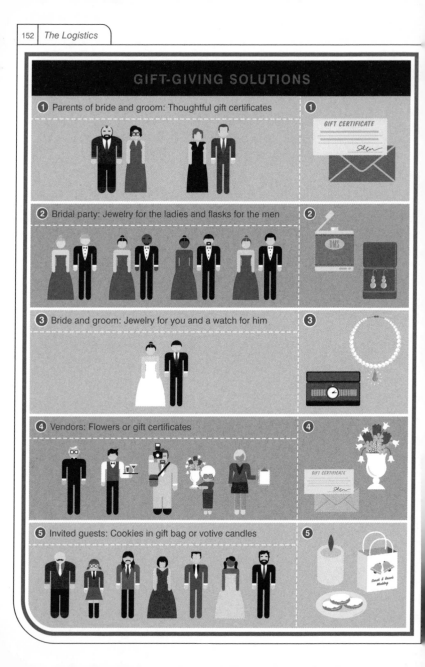

Gifts for Everyone!

Your wedding is not only a time to receive, it's a big time to give. Even if you and your groom are paying for this wedding completely by yourselves (but especially if you're not), your wedding day is a lovely time to thank those most important to you for being there through it all:

■ **Your parents,** for touching up every scraped knee when you were little; for the college tuition; and for being your parents.

■ **Your girlfriends,** for holding you when that mean boy broke up with you in the fifth grade, at lunchtime, for everyone to see; for holding your hair back after your first college frat party; and for standing up for you on your wedding day.

■ **Your vendors,** who worked tirelessly the night before your wedding to make sure everything was just so, and who didn't roll their eyes when you switched from the sea bass to the broiled lobster tails for the fourth time.

Everyone who's been there along the way deserves your thanks—and if you can afford it, a little token to show it. You are free to give your tokens of gratitude to each recipient whenever you find it appropriate, but an easy time to do the gifts to family and friends is at the rehearsal dinner. Simply stand up, explain what each person has meant to you over the years, and present your gift. In the next section, we'll also cover the gifts you and your groom exchange, as well as the all-important wedding favors for your guests.

Your Parents

Good old Mom and Dad. They've put up with and paid for a lot over the years, and it's time to say a big thank you for everything. Give them something you know they'll love and can really use—don't just pluck the two prettiest Champagne flutes off the shelf of the nearest home store and call it a day. Pick out a beautiful silver frame, get it engraved with your wedding date and a sweet message, and insert a cute picture of you and your fiancé—or one of the two of you and your parents. Write them a thoughtful and sincere letter, and slip in a gift certificate for their favorite bed-and-breakfast in the country.

Whatever you do, make sure you do the same thing, or at least something commensurate, for both sets of parents. Though your parents may have paid the whole way, you can't get them a 10-day Alaskan cruise and your new in-laws a nice vase. Make sure your gift is personal, and that you've put in at least a fraction of the effort they put into your whole lives so that they know how grateful you are for all they've done.

The Bridal Party

This is undoubtedly not the first time you've shopped for your girlfriends (though it might be the first time your man has shopped for his dudes). This time, however, you're not just getting your girlfriend that sweater you know she's been eyeing—you're buying her something to say thanks for being there when you were little girls in pigtails, when you became young women, and today, as you say your vows.

A common bridal party tradition is to present each of your bridesmaids with the jewelry she'll wear at your wedding, whether they're all the same or selected pieces you feel fit each one individually (all while seamlessly matching their bridesmaids gowns, of course). You might choose a framed picture of the two of you, an entire album chronicling your friendship, a monogrammed tote she can use long after the wedding, or a gift certificate (enough for your friend and a guest) to her favorite restaurant. There are no rules here—just make sure the gift you give says everything you want it to.

As for your fiancé's guys, well, there's always the list of standard groomsmen gifts that do really work well—such as cufflinks and flasks—but he could also treat them all to a baseball game or some other sports outing. The restaurant gift certificate works for groom's gifts, too.

Each Other

Giving each other gifts on your wedding day is optional because let's face it, this whole day, your wedding bands, and the whole happily-ever-after thing is really your gift to each other. But many couples do like to exchange gifts on their wedding day so that special "something" will always have irreplaceable sentimental value.

It's traditional to have "runners" present the gifts on your behalf the morning of your wedding, just as you're getting ready, so that you don't see each other before the big reveal at the top of the aisle; also frequently included is a letter (re)proclaiming your love for each other. Sound hokey? Yes, it might right now—but sitting at the foot of your bed, with a gorgeous white dress on, reading his handwritten note (which accompanied another lovely piece of jewelry) about how he can't wait to start his life with you, will make you pretty happy you decided to do the gift thing. There are no rules for this gift, either, but a bride's gift of a watch to her groom and a groom's gift of a piece of jewelry are traditions you can't really argue with.

Your Vendors

To whom you give a thank-you gift when it comes to your vendors is entirely up to you. If a vendor's service was excellent, you should write an articulate and praise-filled thank-you note that the vendor can use on his or her Web site as a glowing testimonial. However, if there was a vendor or two, perhaps your planner or florist, with whom you worked extra closely and who really went above and beyond what you perceived to be their duties, go ahead and send them a beautiful arrangement of flowers (if they're *not* your florist, of course!) or a gift certificate to a restaurant. They'll be blown away by your thoughtfulness—but it's only right considering their extra efforts.

Your Guests

This is another aspect of wedding-planning that tends to get lost in the shuffle, but you'll want to thank your guests for coming to your wedding. Place a small token, either at their place setting or on a table from which they can take it on the way out of the reception.

■ Try to come up with something practical. You might think it's darling to compile a CD of all your and your honey's favorite songs, but unless your guests also love John Mayer or 50 Cent, this may not be quite the crowd-pleaser you assume it will be. Ditto for that small silver frame engraved with your wedding date. Much as they love you, it's doubtful they'll be displaying this in their homes, and the engraving makes it impractical for repurposing.
■ Try to come up with something that anyone could use, regardless of gender or age. You could wrap a tiny vanilla-scented candle in a pretty tulle bag with a personalized label saying, "Thanks for celebrating with us! Love, Sarah and Brian." Or get beautifully decorated sugar cookies, shaped and

frosted to look like a wedding cake. Anything edible is noticed, appreciated, and gone in a flash.

Zap Those Bar Codes: It's Registry Time

And speaking of gifts: Somewhere along the party-planning line, you're going to have to register. Yep, as in, pick out all the things you've always dreamed of having in a home of your own one day (stemless wineglasses! Frette linens! A tomato slicer!). If something about this whole process feels a little obnoxious, don't worry. Think of it this way: You'd know what to get your sister when she gets married, and your best friend, and probably a good handful of other close people in your life. You could even pick out their china, and it'd be right on.

But the rest? You know that stress you feel when you have *no idea* what to get people for their birthday or graduation? That's what the majority of your guests will feel like when it comes to buying you and your honey a gift without knowing what you want or need. Registering not only ensures that you'll get at least the types of things you need/want/enjoy for your house, it also takes the burden off your guests when it comes to giving. So don't worry—going crazy with the bar-code gun is actually *not* one of your Bridezilla moments.

Registering is something you should do at least six months ahead. You want to give your guests time to peruse the various stores and price points for the items you've signed up for, and you definitely want to be all set in time for anyone to throw you a surprise shower.

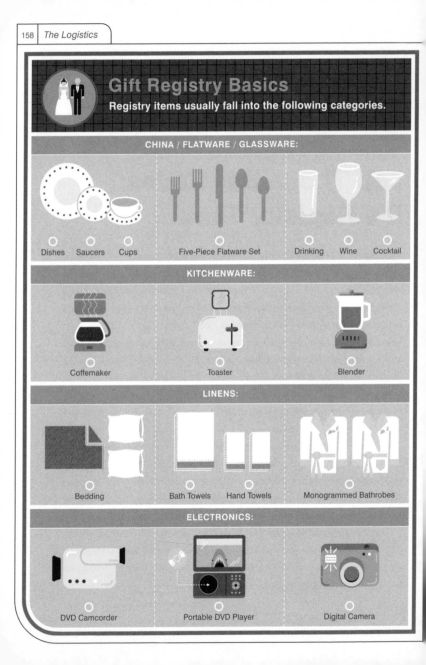

■ Talk with your husband-to-be about the kind of stuff you want. (Are you formal or casual? Are there colors you both love?) Then start hitting up the stores.

■ You'll want to consider kitchen and tableware, linens, china, and maybe even furniture or electronics. You can probably do this in three stores, but there's no rule dictating how many stores you can go to.

■ Word of where you've registered will spread only after about one billion people ask. Your bridesmaids will tell people in time for your shower, and it'll all work out. (You know this already, but *no*, you may not tell people where you've registered via an insert in your formal wedding invitation.)

■ As for getting your groom to come along shopping with you, and be all smiles? That part's up to you.

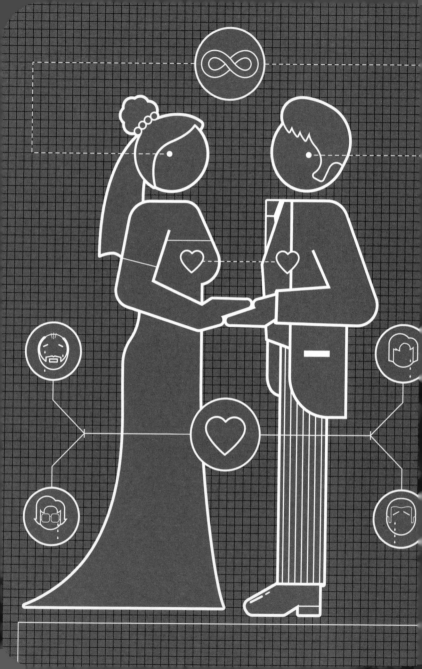

Chapter 8

The Ceremony

With all the fun—and stress and details and planning—that goes into putting together the reception, mapping out the details of your ceremony can almost come as an afterthought. But it shouldn't. This is, after all, the part of the day when you actually become husband and wife. It's where your vows are exchanged, you touch and talk to each other for the first time ever as a married couple—and there's not a dry eye in the house. You need to plan the ceremony with the same care as you took with all your wedding day logistics, but also with the goal of creating a moment when you can truly be "present": basking in the love of your partner, witnessed by the people you love most, you're about to take a step in your life that's truly momentous.

To Involve God or Not to Involve God?

Most likely, by the time you've decided that your partner is the person with whom you want to spend the rest of your life, you'll know what type of marriage ceremony the two of you would have at its most basic level: religious or civil. But if you find yourself not really sure which fits you best as a couple, ask yourselves some questions:

■ Are either you or your fiancé religious? Is it important enough to one or both of you that you'd want to say your vows in a religious setting?
■ Is a religious ceremony something your immediate family will expect?
■ Do you intend to raise a family in a religious household?
■ Do you have strong feelings (either way) when you think of having a religious service?

■ Would you and your fiancé prefer a small civil ceremony, to keep it quick, simple, and intimate, then follow up with a bigger bash for the rest of your friends and family?

■ Timing-wise, would it work better for you to plan a civil ceremony?

Once you know the general direction you're going with your ceremony, the rest will quickly fall into place.

Religious Ceremonies

When planning a religious ceremony, you'll need to understand (if you don't already) the various requirements and restrictions or rules that govern such ceremonies, since these issues will likely impact where your ceremony can take place.

Some examples:

■ If both you and your fiancé are Catholic, you can rule out that sunset ceremony on the beach. In order for a Catholic priest to perform the ceremony, it must take place inside a Catholic church.

■ If you are Catholic but your fiancé is not, you'll need to determine whether a non-church wedding is A-OK according to his religious practice; then your Catholic priest can attend, stand by, and say a blessing while the other officiant presides over the ceremony.

■ Are you both Jewish? If so, be aware that your rabbi will not start a wedding ceremony before sundown on a Saturday. If that's a problem, you better start making calls to venues to check on their Sunday availability.

THE WEDDING CEREMONY: This diagram shows the traditional place

BRIDE'S FAMILY AND GUESTS

...entrance order for everyone in the wedding party.

GROOM'S FAMILY AND GUESTS

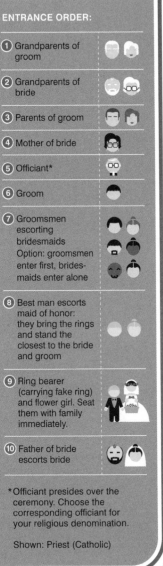

ENTRANCE ORDER:

1. Grandparents of groom

2. Grandparents of bride

3. Parents of groom

4. Mother of bride

5. Officiant*

6. Groom

7. Groomsmen escorting bridesmaids
Option: groomsmen enter first, bridesmaids enter alone

8. Best man escorts maid of honor: they bring the rings and stand the closest to the bride and groom

9. Ring bearer (carrying fake ring) and flower girl. Seat them with family immediately.

10. Father of bride escorts bride

*Officiant presides over the ceremony. Choose the corresponding officiant for your religious denomination.

Shown: Priest (Catholic)

These are just a few examples of the issues that will ultimately affect your choice of ceremony date and venue for the ceremony. Be sure to check with someone in the know (your clergyperson or other religious advisor) so that you have everything straight before you dive in.

Be aware:

■ Just as with your venue, you're going to have to deal with booking dates, negotiating, and putting your name in various places before one comes through. (You can't simply expect that because it's a house of worship there will be no questions asked, no papers to sign, or no deposits to fork over.)

■ You'll need to check about specific rules at your church, synagogue, or ceremony site. Some have dress codes or other restrictions—guests may not blow bubbles as the couple exits due to the film they leave on the hardwood floors, etc. You'll want to know about these before you go ahead and sign.

Finding Your Officiant

If you don't have your own personal priest, rabbi, minister, or other officiant whom you've always known would pronounce you husband and wife (and don't worry, a lot of people don't), start talking.

■ Ask married friends and relatives if they have an officiant they love and would recommend—or if they've attended an area wedding presided over by a great one.

■ If you attend a house of worship, make an appointment to talk to the officiant there.

■ Do your best to get to know him or her so that you have a good comfort level and feel you "click" personality-wise. Nothing makes for a touching nuptial ceremony more than an officiant who really knows the bride and groom. After all, he or she is the one running the show.

Feel free to ask your potential officiant anything you're wondering about, just as you would any other vendor. Besides learning the rules for the ceremony venue, you'll want to ask:

- Does he require pre-wedding counseling (e.g., Pre-Cana in the Catholic religion)? If so, how many sessions?
- Is she all right with your writing your own vows, or must you go with the traditional ones?
- If he needs to travel to the site, does he have any special requirements for how you cover those costs?
- Are you required to pay an honorarium or is it sufficient that you make a contribution to the officiant's congregation?

Once you've decided on a religious ceremony, there's really not a whole lot of wiggle room on the particulars. It's still a good idea to review the entire ceremony from beginning to end with your officiant to make sure the three of you agree on what should happen when and how.

- Make sure you understand the rituals required by your religion and chat about ways to tailor the traditions that are open to interpretation.
- Discuss the choice of music for the procession.
- Review the details of the procession. In the event your parents are divorced, maybe you want both of your parents—and maybe their spouses whom you've known and loved for 20 years—to walk you down the aisle.
- Talk about your vows to get ideas on how best to structure them.
- Review any special blessings or other touches you'd like to add to the cer-

emony: Perhaps you'd like to skip the part where guests are invited to state reasons you shouldn't be united in matrimony, and ask them, instead, to stand up and offer a blessing, prayer, or simply good wishes or advice.

■ Be sure to ask about the paperwork required to make it all "official." Your officiant can direct you to the proper resources for applying for your marriage license, which they will certify for you after the ceremony.

EXPERT TIP: If you and your groom are planning an interfaith ceremony, weaving together two different religions and/or cultures, you may want to choose two officiants, each one representing your and your groom's traditions. Be sure to interview these officiants carefully to determine that they are comfortable acting as "co-officiants." It's vital, too, that they meet each other before the Big Day goes down: You'll want their help to combine different traditions and rituals—and probably readings, music, and blessings—all into one flawless ceremony, which is harder than it may sound. You'll need to make sure all this meshing is allowable by each religion and that you're incorporating elements important to each tradition.

Civil Ceremonies

There are a host of reasons why you and your spouse-to-be may opt to go the civil route, and they don't all have to start with neither of you being religious (though this would clearly be the obvious route if you wanted to keep religion out of it).

■ Perhaps you fell in love on a remote island in the Caribbean and don't feel like dealing with all the paperwork and hoopla your church requires (or with finding a priest amid all the coconut groves).

■ Maybe religion is important to both of you, but you'd rather sidestep the complications of an interfaith ceremony and just do it your way, together.

■ Perhaps having a civil ceremony means that you don't have the venue restrictions you would otherwise have with a religious one.

■ Or maybe you're just not into the whole wedding shebang, and a quickie ceremony—the faster you can call each other husband and wife—sounds all the better to you.

CIVIL WEDDINGS

1 Allow you to have all the usual wedding trappings minus the religious component.

2 Are officiated by a judge, magistrate, or other civil servant.

Whatever your reasons, be aware of two common misconceptions about a civil ceremony:

[1] Just because it's not a religious ceremony doesn't mean you can't have the bridesmaids, the flowers, and the whole package deal, with the only difference being the absence of religion. It doesn't just have to be you, your groom, and a bunch of roses from the corner deli waiting in line outside Room 415 at City Hall.

[2] Just because it's a civil ceremony, do not kid yourselves that this will mean less legwork and fewer logistics: Regulations regarding marriage licenses in your state still apply, and you'll still have to plan ahead, make appointments, file the paperwork, and, of course, find an officiant.

If you haven't already shown your friend how to get ordained online so that he or she may tie your knot (yep, that's really how it works), search for a civil officiant the same way you would a religious one—unless you're going the City Hall route, in which case you'll more than likely meet your judge for the first time as he opens his mouth to greet your dearly beloved and remind them why they've gathered there that day.

Ask around and see who other people have used for a civil ceremony—as long as that person holds the civil title of judge, mayor, justice of the peace, magistrate, county or court clerk, or even notary public, he or she has the power to pronounce you husband and wife.

Speak to the officiant about the same things you would your priest or rabbi—and make sure they know everything you'd like your ceremony to entail, and any way you'd like to put your personal stamp on it. Again, civil only means the absence of religion, so however you want to do this—a

special song during the procession, personally written vows, your favorite aunt reading your favorite poems—is easily accommodated.

The Rehearsal Dinner

The rehearsal dinner takes place the night before the wedding. (Read: No, your bachelor/bachelorette parties should not be on this night.) It's an opportunity for you, your family, and the bridal party to rehearse the ceremony, wherever that may be, and then celebrate afterward with a lovely dinner (and toasts, and toasts, and toasts). This is a great time to present the gifts you've chosen for your loved ones (see page 153); it's also a great time for everyone who loves you to get out those most embarrassing speeches/stories/toasts, etc. (as opposed to during the actual wedding).

Traditionally, the groom's parents pay for this event. Often, your in-laws-to-be are happy to have this opportunity to contribute and add to the festivities. Also traditionally, the event is limited to both sets of parents, the bridal party, and other very close friends and family members who are in from out of town—it's not meant to be a mini-wedding. You'll have a few glasses of wine, a roaring good time—but then, get out of there and get to bed. You're getting married tomorrow!

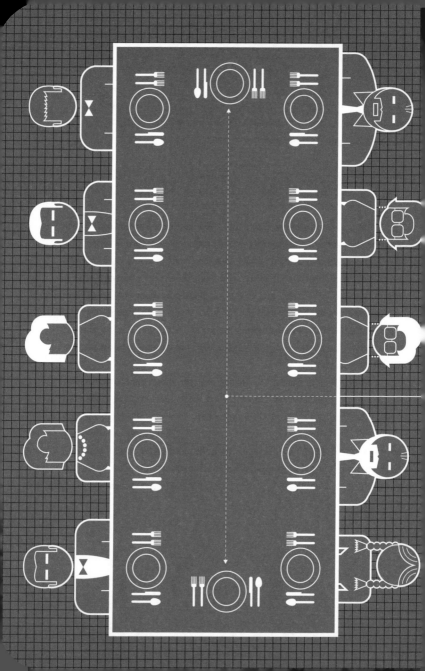

Chapter 9

Managing Relationships:

Control and Maintenance

Planning a wedding involves those people in the world with whom you are the closest: your dear parents (and your fiancé's, who will be dear to you eventually, if they aren't now), your family, your best friends, and, of course, your soul mate/other half/the man with whom you are going to spend the rest of your life.

You might enter into this process thinking this particular group is one with whom you are unlikely to fight constantly—and maybe you won't. Then again, you might be surprised. You know how, when you're stressed or in a bad mood, you tend to take it out on those closest to you, because, well, they still have to love you, even when you're nasty? Such is the case for wedding planning, and when it's actually these people who are *causing* your stress and your bad moods, you might find yourself needing a time out. Here are the relationships where you'll find tensions at their highest. Think of this chapter as a guide to pre-wedding relationship tangles—and how to get out of them without anyone losing their cool.

You + Your Groom

You and your boyfriend used to have a pretty good routine going on: You'd go to work, checking in a few times via e-mail to see how the other's day is going. You'd come home—either to each other or to your own place, and then get together to grab dinner/run errands/watch your favorite shows/see friends/catch a movie/do normal, everyday boyfriend-girlfriend things. Weekends were spent getting coffee and reading newspapers, relaxing, rejuvenating, and attending social events.

Now, you and your *fiancé* go to work, and you send him three e-mails before noon making sure he remembers you're meeting the florist right after work, so he needs to leave a few minutes early, and you both rush to the meeting and get road rage along the way; then at the meeting he rolls his eyes at your deep desire to have orchids covering *every* surface at your wedding; and when you get home, the caterer has sent over your final menu, and once he sees the goat-cheese-and-mushroom phyllo puffs in print, he reneges on his approval, deciding they are actually a bit too frou-frou-y, and that puts you into a tailspin that results in you each going to bed convinced you are marrying a nutcase and wondering if it'd really be *that bad* if you gave/got the ring back.

And weekends? Ooh. Jam-packed. And yes, you guessed it—not with relaxing, rejuvenating, and social events, but with appointments, wedding-related errands, and decision-making.

There may be some slight exaggeration here, of course, but you get the idea. All of a sudden, there's this huge *thing* that was never a part of your relationship before. And it's not just a little thing—a wedding brings with it high, intense emotions circling around a few very sensitive subjects: family, money, and the most important day of your life. All of a sudden, you have to work together to make all kinds of decisions—incessant decisions—and when you don't agree on them, you bicker. And bickering can lead to fighting, and fighting can lead to, well, *questioning*.

If this sounds like you, relax. This is normal. It happens. And since you're aware of it, take advantage of your moment of clarity. Chances are, you'll realize you need a break after you've gone in circles for hours about what song you'll make your entrance to at your reception, and that your life/conversations/relationship shouldn't be all wedding, all the time.

So, take a break: Have a date night—one where the slightest mention of anything concerning the wedding is off-limits. Or make it a whole weekend. Not talking about the wedding at all for a while will bring you back to the way your relationship once was—the way it will be again *after* your wedding. Soon, you'll remember why you're marrying this person, and why he truly is the person you want to spend the rest of your life with.

Defining Your Groom Type

Wedding-detail-related bickering aside, there's some other behavior your groom might exhibit during the wedding-planning time that may make you want to throttle him, despite the fact that the ring on your left finger is the prettiest thing you've ever seen. Most behavior can be categorized into the following two types.

Type A—He Isn't Doing Squat:

■ He agrees to everything you say—with a beer in his left hand, the remote in his right, his eyes, unblinking, staring at the game, and in the most indifferent, dismissive tone you've probably ever heard.

■ He's late to appointments (after whining about going to them).

■ He is unwilling to actually sit down with you and put together this and that list—and it's starting to exhaust you.

What to do? Try to figure out something that wouldn't be completely painful for him to be involved in—and therefore not completely painful for you to *try* to get him involved in. If you two have already decided you want a tropical beach locale for your honeymoon and he loves to travel, ask him to look into various destinations, hotels, and honeymoon packages. That way, something that really needs to get done is getting done; and now he can't moan about it and add to your already mounting stress.

TYPE A GROOM—DOING NOTHING

1. Mindlessly agrees with everything you say
2. Late to wedding-related appointments
3. Unwilling to sit down with you and figure out wedding lists

TYPE B GROOM—DOING TOO MUCH

4. Nitpicks wedding details
5. Nags you about your to-do list
6. Wastes too much time deciding on tux for himself and groomsmen

DEFINING YOUR GROOM

Some grooms do very little, and others do too much.

Type B—His Secret Martha Side Rears Its Ugly Head:

■ You expected your guy would be a Type A (or at least a variation on the most common male wedding-planning stereotype), but all of a sudden he's piping up about just what shade of blue *he* thinks the fondant on your cake should be—and you didn't exactly ask.

■ Suddenly, he's asking you probing questions about what you have and haven't gotten done yet.

■ He's taking an inordinate amount of time to choose his tux and the groomsmen's formal wear (and not because he's procrastinating—because he's pondering the wondrous differences between various tail lengths and trim fabrics) and generally standing in the way of your crossing that task off your list.

Thought you'd just kind of slap this thing together without having to ask his opinion on everything you sign? First of all—be grateful! He wants to be involved! He cares! Gripe too much about this, and you'll have other brides lining up to take a sock at you. Be happy, warm, and fuzzy that your guy wants to have a say in your wedding day—and then, ever so gently, if you're starting to feel like he's in your hair just a bit, *give him a job*.

■ Pick something you know he'd be great at, and hand it over. But *really* hand it over—give it to him completely, and don't nag.

■ Ask him to pick the band—and then stand back and let him narrow down your options, then invite you out to see his favorite three.

■ You'll need at least two hotel options for out-of-town guests—have him look up some good ones, research prices, block off rooms, and just pass along the info to you by the time your stationer needs it.

Truly, it's great that he wants to be involved. Let him.

You + Your Bridesmaids

They're your best friends. Your sisters. Your fiancé's sisters. The cousins and former roommates with whom you are closest. Surely they couldn't cause you any headaches or stress during the happiest months of your life, right?

Think hard. Though you may love these people with everything you've got, they're also probably a bunch who can press your buttons better than most (because they *so* know what they are), and who have an uncanny ability to get under your skin. Consider these scenarios:

■ Your best friend is oohing and ahhing at the dress you've chosen for her to try on, but the way her eyes keep flitting over to the corner, you can tell she'd really rather be stepping into the navy halter she spied when you first walked in. *Worth confronting her about*, in a fit of frustration, as the salon's seamstress is measuring her bust? Probably not.

■ Your best friend oohs and ahhs at the dress you've chosen for her to try on, and then you turn around for a second and she emerges from the dressing room in the navy halter she spied when she first walked in, just as a suggestion (you know, in case the eye-flitting didn't make it clear just how much better she likes her choice).
Worth confronting her about? This is an instance where you should feel free, nicely, to assert your bridaldom and declare *your* choice to be *the* choice.

Whenever the potential for a little tiff arises, you're going to have to apply the discriminating knowledge of when to pick your battles. You know these people best, and you know how best to handle them and any issues that may come with them—and thus, in some cases, how to head them off.

PROBLEM BRIDESMAID: If a troublesome bridesmaid's behavior starts t

POTENTIAL BRIDESMAID PROBLEMS THAT MAY REQUIRE FIRING:

1. Absent from scheduled bridesmaid events and festivities
2. Balks at paying expenses (dress, travel, etc.)
3. Engages in inappropriate behavior at engagement party
4. Not complying with mandatory dress code

big day and talking with her doesn't work, don't be afraid to send her packing.

You probably know, before you even ask her to be a bridesmaid, which friend is going to snort at the various costs of standing up for you that day. If legitimate concerns are behind her whining, offer to help ahead of time. Tell her you know being a bridesmaid is expensive, and that her dress is going to be your gift to her. It's a nice gesture, it'll show her how much you really do want her to be a part of your wedding, and, in the end, it will probably save a fight. You'd probably be able to hear only so much of her whining before you wondered if she hated how much this was costing her more than she wanted to be there for you on your wedding day.

Firing Your Bridesmaid

If all attempts at staving off silly bickering fail, and all attempts at having calm, mature sit-downs should any real problematic issues arise aren't making things better, can you fire your bridesmaid?

This is a personal judgment call, but unless you're willing to lose the friendship over her sucky job as your bridesmaid, you should try your best *not* to fire her. However, If you're getting the sense she's wishing she hadn't said yes pretty much the same way you're questioning why you ever asked her, give her the easy out:

■ Have a conversation with her about how difficult being in your wedding is for her.

■ Let her bring up the reasons she's having a tough time of it: the cost, the traveling, etc.

■ More often than not, you'll end up on the same page, and you'll come to the mutual realization that she should not be your bridesmaid.

In the end, it's always good to talk things out. You may not realize that the bad breakup she went through six months before you got engaged is unexpectedly rearing its ugly head in the form of sadness, jealously, or panic at your impending nuptials. She may have recent financial troubles she hasn't shared with anyone. Remember that she's still your friend (or sister or cousin, etc.). There's no reason that shouldn't still be the case after your I-dos.

You + The Parents (Both Sets)

Let's just go ahead and assume you have experienced conflict with your parents before. From the fit you used to throw every time there was a new My Little Pony you wanted, to the time you brought home that deadbeat punk (a phase you went through before you found *him*), you and your parents have undoubtedly been through it all.

On one hand, that's a good thing, because it means that, during the wedding whirl, you're not going to go through anything with them you probably haven't seen before, in one form or another. You probably already know your mom is going to be a nutcase over the containers holding the centerpieces, and you probably already know your dad will somehow justify the ridiculously expensive cabernet he feels should be served with the filet but balk at your need to have the Jimmy Choos with exactly the same crystal detailing as your already costly dress.

But then, there are your groom's parents. They can present a whole new set of issues. Issues you haven't grown up with—issues that you weren't expecting to come out or that you didn't even know existed. You can't deal with your in-laws-to-be the same way you handle your own parents. And, as we've talked about before, a wedding is one of those "happy" life events that brings out some of the most divisive issues and packs them all into one nice, neat, horrifying little package: family, money, appearances, and each and every single person's perceived right to be in control.

Presenting a United Front

Whether or not you expect your wedding planning to turn into World War III, it's a good idea, before you sit down with either set of parents, to hash out a few details—the basics—with just a party of two.

Most of this was covered in the first chapters, but it's worth emphasizing that at the outset of all your planning, you and your groom should sit down and talk about the type of wedding you want.

[1] The general size and atmosphere (totally casual in a restaurant or backyard vs. a grand affair in a ballroom)

[2] The time of year

[3] The number of attendants you each want

[4] How lavish or informal you're picturing this event to be

And then, for all the remaining issues you're uncertain about—or all those inevitable things to come that you know you can't even begin to guess about right now—*agree to always be a team*.

Don't say yes to anything (to any parents or vendors) without first checking with the other. That way, when your parents start talking about how they've already reserved X, Y, and Z dates at the country club your father plays golf at every Sunday, and the two of you have decided you'd love to look into your favorite museum in the city where you met and fell in love, not only can you say, "No thanks, Mom and Dad," you can say that the two of you have already discussed it, and a country club wedding is truly not what either of you has in mind.

Most of the time, you'll be pleasantly surprised by their reaction. If they hadn't already, this whole impending marriage thing will probably make your parents realize that you're adults now—and they'll need to respect your carefully thought-out and articulated wishes. Go with this plan, *consistently*, throughout the entire wedding process, and you should be able to steer over bumps without too much wear and tear.

Dealing with Your Parents

So, you entered into this thing thinking hey, my parents are pretty cool, I'm sure this will be smooth sailing. But then, when your mom acts like serving chicken at the reception instead of fish is the most classless thing she's ever heard of, it starts to become clear that she actually may care what other people think of this party she's throwing. And, all of a sudden, your dad seems a little awkward around your fiancé and starts acting like the surly, protective father that he really never was.

Your parents are fallible, too, even if you've never thought of them that way, and your getting married could very well be blowing their parental minds. Whether they're behaving in a way that you were totally ready for or that seems completely out of left field, always be sure to talk about it with them. It's the easiest way to make decisions together,

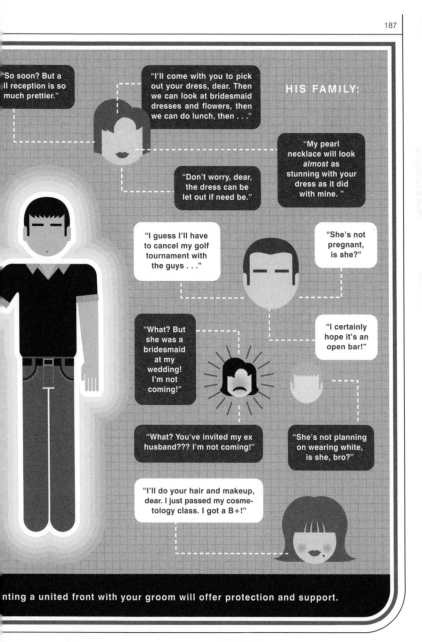

and to figure out if these issues are just silly trifles or real concerns. You do not want anything unresolved to erupt, volcano-style, all over your lovely wedding. You never know what intense emotions and several glasses of Champagne will do. And it's best to keep wondering.

And then there's the money. Oh, right. *That*. If your parents are financing this wedding—in part or in whole—that can add a whole new ingredient to the pot. You think it's your wedding, so it's your way. They think, it's their signatures on the checks, so it's their way. Before you even knock on their door to show them that new rock on your hand, just accept that all of you are going to have to make concessions because, when it comes to your wedding, it turns out *both* of these assumptions are true.

Now you're going to have to decide up-front how you'll navigate this minefield.

■ The easiest thing is to figure out what you care about most, which will help you figure out how to pick your battles when you're all gathered around the kitchen table with estimates and quotes from vendors in hand.

■ If you and your fiancé are foodies, and you absolutely will not skimp on the food—from the butlered hors d'oeuvres to the crème brulée served alongside the cake—then make a sacrifice on another budget item (or pony up some money toward it yourselves, if your parents can't or won't budge on the catering budget).

■ Did you think it would be really nice to have a live band, but your parents keep pointing out it's about $8,000 cheaper to get a good DJ? Maybe that's a good place to give.

Whatever the give and take, always be sure to talk things through with your financiers, so it's always clear where everyone's coming from. Everything will go a whole lot smoother if it's all on the table. So get ready to talk.

Dealing with His Parents

When it comes to your own parents, it's good to have your fiancé by your side because it's important that your parents see you acting as one entity—especially when it comes to making decisions. Still, you don't necessarily *need* your fiancé there, since they're your parents, and you know how to deal with them.

But when it comes to your groom's parents (and his family as a whole), remember that he knows best how to deal with them. Just because you're the bride and are at the helm of this planning business doesn't mean you should dive into issues with your in-laws the same way you dove into picking out the perfect shade of calla lilies. These waters are murkier than the ones you've navigated with your own parents, and you'll need your groom's assistance. Dealing with them as a soon-to-be daughter-in-law is quite different from dealing with them as simply "the girlfriend."

■ Maybe his mom used to fawn all over you, but now that you're actually marrying her only son, she's acting a little weird and territorial and you don't really know what to make of her snippiness.

■ Maybe his mom used to fawn all over you—and now, just as you expected, her fawning is giving you panic attacks because you don't *want* to be taken out for lunch and dress shopping for the past seven Saturdays since you two got engaged.

■ Maybe you don't *want* to wear her veil, but she didn't really even ask— she just cried and beamed as she got it out of storage and presented it to you. If it was your mom, you'd probably be gentle, but maybe you also wouldn't sweat over telling her you have your heart set on a mantilla in the window of the prettiest bridal shop in town. But with her? How are you going to do that?

Relax. Talk to your fiancé. No matter what's going on—a situation you're unsure how to get out of, an offer you'd prefer to decline, an attack you feel was an ambush—talk to him first about how best to deal with it and then, if possible, deal with it together. If you'd rather confront a sticky situation solo, so it doesn't feel like you ratted, that's fine (and maybe a calm sit-down with just you and his parents—or mom—is best). Simply go to him for guidance before you do so. It can help you understand what's behind the situation you're dealing with, and how best to broach the subject with his parents.

Dealing with Various Other Family Members

Try these scenarios on for size:

■ You've really never been your fiancé's sister's number one fan, and when she asked you to be in her wedding two years ago, you were surprised, but did it anyway, grumbling only ever so slightly. But now you realize you might be in a scary place: *Does she have to be one of your bridesmaids? You hate her!*

■ You love your brother to death, but he has a tendency to knock 'em back, especially at these large, open-bar, family-type functions. He's one of your honey's groomsmen, and although he's not the best man, you *just know* he's going to get up and give a speech. And you just know he'll be bombed as he clambers up to the stage to deliver it. He's had a rough few years, so when you bring up your concern to your parents, they brush it off and tell you to leave him alone—*he's your bother and he loves you*. But no amount of love is going to prevent him from telling some extremely embarrassing story about your youthful indiscretions.

■ Your fiancé has one niece—that's it—and you have about a billion nieces and nephews. It'd be difficult to choose among them for your flower girl, and you've known his niece since, well, before she was even born, so you just go ahead and ask her to be your flower girl. But then your sisters are *not happy*. Their munchkins are your blood, and you didn't pick them? *How could you?*

We're not about to talk about anything new here. When it comes to conflicts or heading off potential conflicts with family members, it's best to talk to them up-front—once you've enlisted some support beforehand. Maybe, as it turns out, your fiancé still doesn't know why his sister asked you to be in her wedding, and he bets she would be just fine not being your bridesmaid. Maybe you're pretty good buddies with your brother's best friend, and this buddy will be at the wedding to keep an eye on your brother and make sure he doesn't grab the mic after a few too many. Maybe your mom can explain to your sisters that you just couldn't pick among all your own darling nieces, so they will be asked to bring up the gifts during the ceremony, while your new husband's only pint-sized relative will be scattering the petals that day.

As always, talk, talk, talk—and do it sooner rather than later. These people love you. Give them the benefit of the doubt and let them show how much they care.

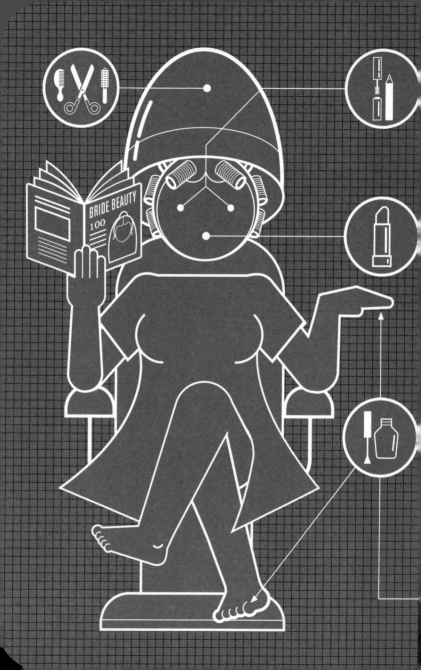

[Chapter 10]

Getting Dress Ready

The dates are set, the roles have been cast, all of your logistics have been put into motion. Now you can return to the really important stuff—you, and what you'll look like in The Dress.

You probably don't even need to read this section, as you've already booked a 255-pound jacked personal trainer for 5:45 A.M. from now until the day before the wedding, and you have standing appointments at all the best spas and salons. (Right?) And, it's true, even when you're buried under day-of transportation details and busy compiling a guest list, your ongoing quest to be wedding-day ready will never be far from your mind.

That's fine—and normal—but try not to make yourself nuts. Remember, the person you'll most care about that day would think you were gorgeous even if you wore a potato sack and the headband you wear only when you're washing your face. Nevertheless, here's an easy way to break down your physical preparations prior to and on the big day.

Toning Up That Bod

Brides invariably fall prey to the desire to shed a few pounds in their efforts to be dress-ready. The good news: Chances are, you've got some time before you strut down that aisle, which means you can lose weight slowly and gradually, the most effective (and healthy) way.

[1] Break down the amount of time before your wedding and the amount of weight you want to lose, then decide how best to tackle it.

[2] Research various aided diets (Weight Watchers, etc.) or talk to a nutritionist or your health-nut friend to get advice, tips, and maybe even a plan for slimming down in the coming months.

[**3**] If you haven't already, join a gym. And once you're in that gym, don't just get on the treadmill with the current *Us Weekly* and zone out. Look into classes, personal training sessions, or even programs specifically geared toward brides-to-be who want to buff up before they step into their Vera Wang.

[**4**] Ask your personal trainer—or scour issues of *Self*, *Shape*, and *Women's Health*—for the exercises that will tone your arms, back, abs, bum, thighs, and calves. Your dress is sure to show off at least one of these aspects—and your honeymoon will undoubtedly bare them all.

Sustained Grooming

As you're carving out your deltoids and taking inches off your thighs, it's also a good idea to start getting in shape everything on your surface. You may already go to a stylist regularly to get your hair cut and colored, and maybe you have someone you trust as a facialist, too. Talk to them: Tell them what you want your hair, teeth, and skin to look like in X number of months, and they can help you figure out how to do it.

Hair

You know how you usually wait four months—until you've got quadruple ends you pick apart when you're bored—before having your hair trimmed? If you want shampoo-commercial locks on your wedding day, your stylist will probably advise against this habit. Talk with her about regular trims, deep-conditioning treatments, and the timing of such treatments as highlights to make sure your hair on your wedding day resembles all those lofty visions in your head.

⚠ EXPERT TIP: Any good stylist will tell you not to make drastic changes to your hair before your wedding. When you get your proofs back from the photographer, you'll want to gaze on the glowing vision of you at your finest—instead of glaring at those half grown-out experimental bangs.

Teeth

So, you talked your parents out of torturing you with braces when you were sixteen years old—but now, with bajillions of pictures about to be snapped of you and your smile, you kind of wish you had taken care of that snaggle tooth. And your three-cups-of-coffee-a-day habit is staring back at you in the mirror in the form of some not-so-bright chompers.

Add your dentist to the list of people to notify about your engagement—now—and talk about what's possible to fix or enhance in the time before your wedding. These days, there are all sorts of options for straightening and whitening (from at-home kits to quick in-office treatments), so you'll be ready to flash your hundred-watt smile.

Nails

Until you get closer to your wedding date, it's unnecessary to start having regular manicures to get your nails in shape. Unless, of course you're a biter. In which case, you should at the very least start painting your nails every two weeks so that you keep them out of your mouth.

⚠ EXPERT TIP: For your day-of-wedding mani and pedi, chances are you're imagining getting those treatments surrounded by your bridal party, and probably both the moms, at a lovely, relaxing, pampering, calm-inducing spa. It's the perfect way to keep your jitters down (by surrounding yourself

with your favorite chatty women), look polish-perfect, and have a fun little girl-bonding session before walking down the aisle. Just make sure you send out an e-mail blast to all the ladies in question a few weeks ahead of time, asking them if they would all be free, verifying that the prices at your chosen spa are OK with them (unless, of course, you've decided to treat), and ensuring they don't just go ahead and get their manicures three days before your wedding day.

Skin

As soon as possible, book appointments for the best facialist at your favorite spa or with your dermatologist—and preferably both. Regular visits with each will keep your regular skin problems (dryness, acne, etc.) in check and let you devise a plan for combating them as your wedding day approaches.

Trial Visits

All your months-before preparations are great—but consultations with the individuals who will be doing your hair and makeup the day of the wedding are critical for ensuring that you'll like the way you look as you step into that dress.

For both your hair and your makeup, set up an appointment several weeks before the wedding with the people who will be beautifying you. At this trial run, they will do for you exactly what you'll want them to do the day of your wedding: full hair and makeup, veil, false eyelashes and all. You'll want to see what works: Maybe you always pictured a loose, off-center chignon—and at your trial run, you discover that it's

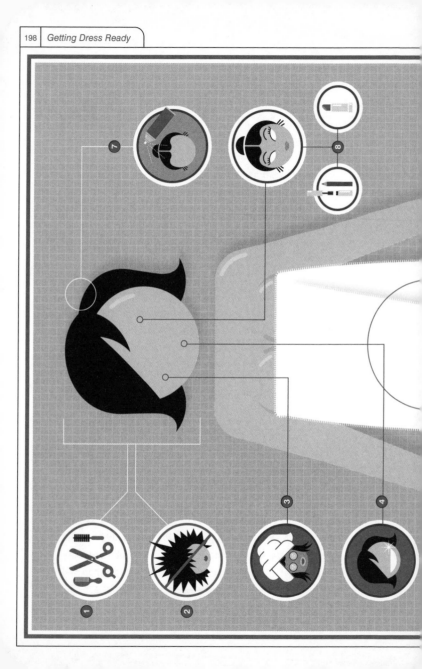

START PREPARING MONTHS BEFORE THE WEDDING

HAIR:

1. Get regular trims
2. Avoid drastic hairstyle changes

SKIN:

3. Get regular facials

TEETH:

4. Consult your dentist about whitening and straightening

FIGURE:

5. Start a diet plan
6. Start an exercise routine

SET UP TRIAL VISITS SEVERAL WEEKS BEFORE WEDDING TO TEST:

7. Hairstyle
8. Makeup

DAY OF WEDDING:

9. Manicure and pedicure

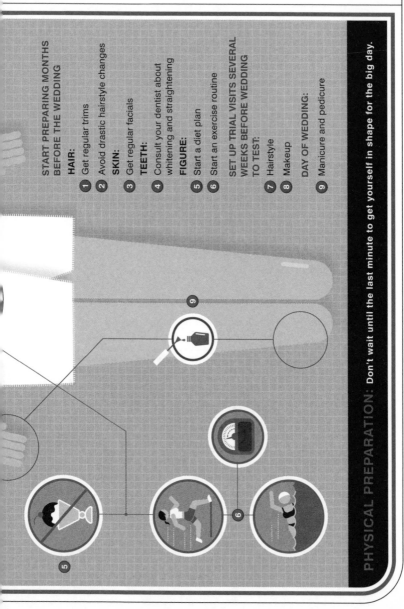

PHYSICAL PREPARATION: Don't wait until the last minute to get yourself in shape for the big day.

absolutely gorgeous from the back but doesn't look too much different from the usual thrown-back-in-a-bun look you sport almost every day, so you decide you'd like something different. Or maybe you want a smoky eye, but it actually takes a while to figure out if it will be a violet or navy or grayish smoky eye.

Your trial run is where you figure this all out. If you leave it till the hour before your father is supposed to give you away, it's pretty safe to say you should build in time for a super-soaker meltdown.

[1] As you did before you went dress shopping, gather ideas for the looks you like: Rip pictures from magazines and print images from the Web of hairstyles and makeup looks you love.

[2] Bring your look book to the people who will be responsible for re-creating them: your hair stylist and makeup artist.

AVOID A POTENTIAL DISASTER BY SCHEDULING A TRIAL RUN FOR YOUR HAIR AND MAKEUP AHEAD OF TIME.

DISASTROUS

1 Hair too big and oversprayed
2 Brows are overdrawn
3 Eyeshadow too dark and false lashes too thick
4 Blush too heavy
5 Lipstick too dark

PERFECTION

[3] Then, at your trial run, talk to your consultant about the best way to achieve your look, taking into consideration your veil or headpiece, overall style, the type of wedding you're having, the environment that day, and what will actually work for you.

For example, if your stylist knows that your superfine tresses will not hold a curl if you're planning to wear your hair down for your beach ceremony, he can break it to you well in advance, as opposed to the morning of your wedding. The same goes for your makeup artist: If your everyday routine includes blotting your shiny zones before noon and you'd rather not have a compact shoved down your dress the day of your wedding, your makeup artist can figure out the best plan of attack—as well as determine that perfect shade of smoky eye.

Hello, Gorgeous

Above all, if you take away just one thing from this chapter, please let it be the image of you in your potato sack on page 194. Seriously. This is definitely the best dress you've ever worn, and maybe—unless you've got an Oscar invite up your sleeve—it's the best dress you will ever wear. Your hair and makeup will be professionally done, yes, and there's no doubt you'll be wearing some lovely jewels in addition to the rock your guy gave you roughly a year ago.

But above all, you know deep in your heart that he won't remember the specifics of your sweetheart neckline or empire waist. He'll only remember that he's never seen you look so beautiful, radiant, and glowing.

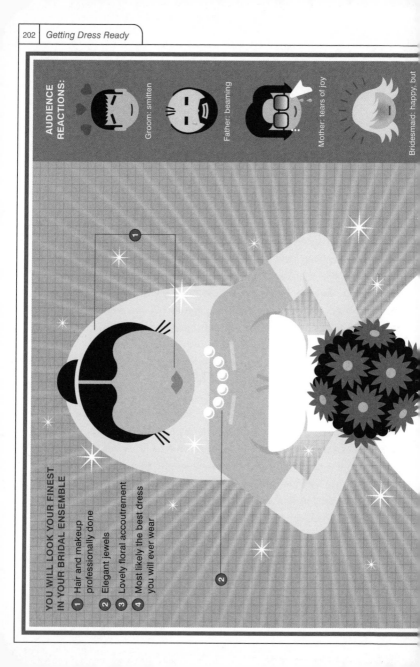

YOU WILL LOOK YOUR FINEST IN YOUR BRIDAL ENSEMBLE

1. Hair and makeup professionally done
2. Elegant jewels
3. Lovely floral accoutrement
4. Most likely the best dress you will ever wear

AUDIENCE REACTIONS:

Groom: smitten

Father: beaming

Mother: tears of joy

Bridesmaid: happy, but

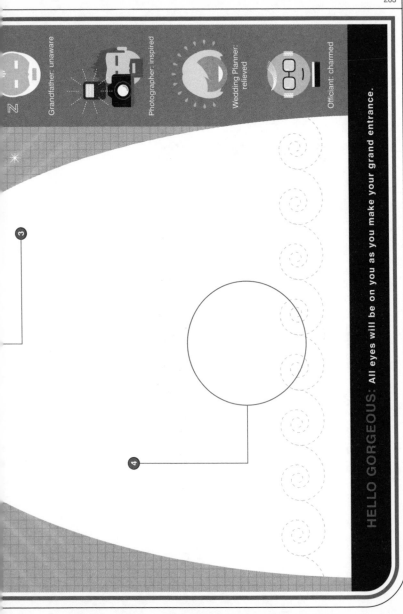

HELLO GORGEOUS: All eyes will be on you as you make your grand entrance.

Grandfather: unaware

Photographer: inspired

Wedding Planner: relieved

Officiant: charmed

203

Conclusion:

When It's All Said and Done—
You're Married!

Soon, this book will be a thing of the past. Soon, you won't be a mere girlfriend or fiancée anymore. You'll be a wife. You'll be tan—from that fabulous honeymoon, of course. And you'll have all sorts of wonderful time now that you don't need to worry about appointments and fabric swatches and cake tastings.

But just to make sure your entry back into reality isn't too harsh, here are a few tips on the one last task you have to accomplish to wrap up this wedding: your thank-you notes.

Giving Thanks: A How-To

If you lay the proper groundwork, your thank-you notes should be an easy job to square away. A few basics:

[1] Despite what you may have heard, you do not have a year to complete them. Eight weeks is actually pushing it for getting your thank-you notes out the door for gifts you received before or just after the wedding. Do whatever you have to do to make sure that happens. Your guests deserve it.

[2] If your budget allows, have your stationer print out another set of envelopes on your chosen thank-you-note stationery when you print your invitations. Then, that tedious and dreaded part of addressing a million envelopes will already be done. Maybe you won't use a few, but even your declined RSVPs will probably send a gift at some point, and you'll nearly die of relief when you find how convenient it is to have your envelopes ready to go.

[3] Printed envelopes or not, it's a good idea to bring your address list and note cards on the honeymoon. To do over a candlelit dinner on the beach? C'mon. But, especially if you've got a long flight, imagine how happy you'll be when you land at home and you and your new hubby have them all done. It's the perfect thing to do on a plane—and it's not like you

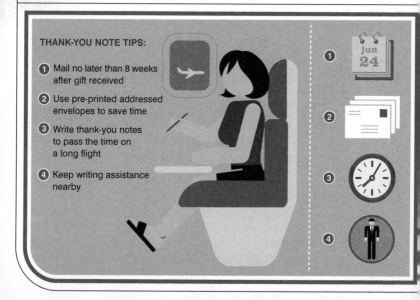

THANK-YOU NOTE TIPS:

1. Mail no later than 8 weeks after gift received
2. Use pre-printed addressed envelopes to save time
3. Write thank-you notes to pass the time on a long flight
4. Keep writing assistance nearby

can get to honeymoon activities until you reach your destination. Added bonus: In the confines of an airplane, your (probably) reluctant husband won't be able to escape writing duty.

And speaking of your (probably) reluctant husband's writing duty, make sure that it's equal to yours. This job can take a while, so get in the swing of the whole new marriage-is-a-partnership-thing and split them up:

■ You should write to your friends and family, and he should write to his friends and family.

■ Thank them profusely for both their presence and their gift; tell them how you plan to use the gift (whether it's a roasting pan or a big, fat check); and mention again how wonderful the day was for you.

■ The note shouldn't be formulaic, but after a few, you'll get the hang of it, and before you know it, they'll all be signed, sealed, and delivered.

Plans for this last task aside, you should be feeling pretty good right now. You're totally ready for your big day—physically, emotionally, and mentally. You're ready to stop thinking about this as a huge undertaking, and ready to just get married.

Because that's what all this is about, you know: Not a day. Not a party. But a marriage. The rest of your life. And that's what you should be focusing on—the fun of it, the joy of it. So get ready to dive in—the time has finally arrived!

[Appendix]

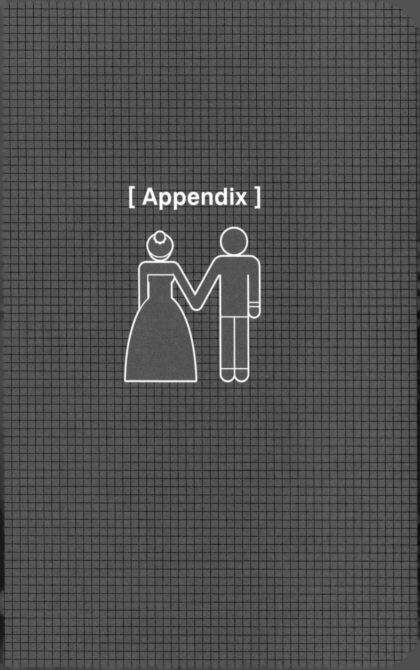

Budget Cheat Sheet
Use this form to track all possible expenditures for your wedding day festivities.

OVERALL BUDGET AVAILABLE

	Venue	$
	Catering	$
	Photographer	$
	Dress	$
	Invitations	$
	Flowers	$
	Transportation	$
	Music	$
	Extras	$
	TOTAL	$

Budget Cheat Sheet

Use this form to track all possible expenditures for your wedding day festivities.

OVERALL BUDGET AVAILABLE

	Venue	$
	Catering	$
	Photographer	$
	Dress	$
	Invitations	$
	Flowers	$
	Transportation	$
	Music	$
	Extras	$
	TOTAL	$

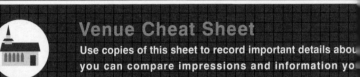

Venue Cheat Sheet

Use copies of this sheet to record important details abou
you can compare impressions and information yo

VENUE

| Name | Date visited | ☐☐ / ☐☐ / ☐ |

Address (Number and Street) | City

State/Province | Country | Zip/Postal Code

TEL ☐☐☐ – ☐☐☐ – ☐☐☐☐ | Web site

COORDINATOR/MANAGER

MR. ○   MS. ○

TEL ☐☐☐ – ☐☐☐ – ☐☐☐☐ | E-mail

Comments

ue choices for your wedding. Once you've visited your top contenders,
rded for each site.

CAPACITY

eremony	Cocktails	( ) YES ( ) NO
inner(seated)	Dance floor	
ours [ ][ ] : [ ][ ] — [ ][ ] : [ ][ ]		

CATERING

n-site	Preferred list	
ee, if bringing in own? $[ ][ ][ ]	Includes cake	( ) YES ( ) NO
cludes table and chairs ( ) YES ( ) NO	Includes table linens	( ) YES ( ) NO

XTRAS

te for photographs ( ) YES ( ) NO	On-site Parking	( ) YES ( ) NO
estrictions	Bridal Room	
own Payment $[ ][ ][ ]	Down Payment to Reserve	$[ ][ ][ ]
verall Impressions		

Drafting the Guest List

After you decide how many nonnegotiable guests will atte
for potential "B" List Guests.

"A" LIST GUESTS

(A) TOTAL GUEST CAPACITY		TOTAL [ ][ ][ ]

(B) NONNEGOTIABLE GUESTS		

BRIDE'S	Family	[ ][ ][ ]
	Friends	[ ][ ][ ]
GROOM'S	Family	[ ][ ][ ]
	Friends	[ ][ ][ ]
CHILDREN INVITED	○ Y ○ N	[ ][ ][ ]

Add up all nonnegotiable guests	TOTAL [ ][ ][ ]

$$(A) - (B) = (C)$$

(C) SEATING AVAILABLE FOR FOR "B" LIST GUESTS & RISKY INVITEES	TOTAL [ ][ ][ ]

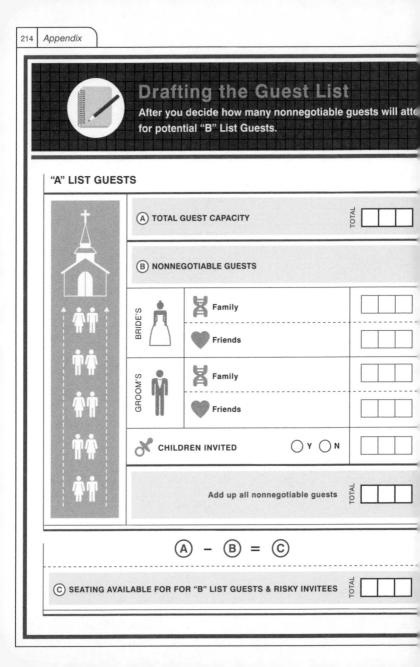

hart below will help you determine how many slots you have available

BRIDE AND GROOM'S "B" LIST GUESTS

Her Friends				His Friends			
Her Co-Worker(s)				His Co-worker(s)			
Her Boss				His Boss			
TOTAL				TOTAL			

PARENTS' "B" LIST GUESTS

	Distant Relatives					Distant Relatives			
BRIDE'S PARENTS	Friends				GROOM'S PARENTS	Friends			
	Boss/Co-Workers					Boss/Co-Workers			
	TOTAL					TOTAL			

⚠ RISKY INVITEES (consider carefully before inviting)

◯ Divorced Friends ◯ him ◯ her

◯ Bride's Ex

◯ Groom's Ex

◯ Tipsy McSwagger

◯ Troublemakers

◯ Misc.

Wedding Planner Cheat Sheet

Use these sheets to help choose your wedding planner. Once y

WEDDING PLANNER

MR. MS.
○ ○

Interview:

DATE ☐☐ / ☐☐ / ☐☐   TIME ☐☐ : ☐☐   ○ A.
                                              ○ P.

Address (Number and Street)   City

State/Province   Country   Zip/Postal Code

TEL ☐☐☐ – ☐☐☐ – ☐☐☐☐   ○ HOME ○ WORK
                                 ○ CELL ○ FAX

Web site   Familiar with venue ○ YE
                                         ○ N

Package includes   Price $ ☐☐☐☐

We clicked/didn't click

your choice, keep his or her contact information close to hand at all times.

WEDDING PLANNER

MR. MS.
◯ ◯

Interview: DATE ☐☐ / ☐☐ / ☐☐   TIME ☐☐ : ☐☐   ◯ A.M. ◯ P.M.

Address (Number and Street)   City

State/Province   Country   Zip/Postal Code

TEL ☐☐☐ – ☐☐☐ – ☐☐☐☐   ◯ HOME ◯ WORK   ◯ CELL ◯ FAX

Web site   Familiar with venue ◯ YES ◯ NO

Package includes   Price $ ☐☐☐☐☐

We clicked/didn't click

Photographer Cheat Sheet

Use these sheets to help choose your wedding photographer. Once y

PHOTOGRAPHER

MR. ○ MS. ○

Interview: DATE [ ] / [ ] / [ ]

Address (Number and Street) | City

State/Province | Country | Zip/Postal Code

TEL [ ][ ][ ] – [ ][ ][ ] – [ ][ ][ ][ ]
○ HOME   ○ WORK
○ CELL   ○ FAX

Web site | Email

Hours | Number of Shots | Price $ [ ][ ][ ][ ]

SECOND PHOTOGRAPHER

MR. ○ MS. ○

TEL [ ][ ][ ] – [ ][ ][ ] – [ ][ ][ ][ ]
○ HOME   ○ WORK
○ CELL   ○ FAX

E-mail | Price $ [ ][ ][ ][ ]

your choice, keep his or her contact information close to hand at all times.

HOTOGRAPHER

R. MS.
◯ ◯

Interview: DATE ☐☐ / ☐☐ / ☐☐

dress (Number and Street)

City

ate/Province

Country

Zip/Postal Code

TEL ☐☐☐ – ☐☐☐ – ☐☐☐☐

◯ HOME ◯ WORK
◯ CELL ◯ FAX

eb site

Email

ours

Number of Shots

Price $ ☐☐☐☐☐

ECOND PHOTOGRAPHER

R. MS.
◯ ◯

TEL ☐☐☐ – ☐☐☐ – ☐☐☐☐

◯ HOME ◯ WORK
◯ CELL ◯ FAX

mail

Price $ ☐☐☐☐☐

Index

About the Author

Although as of press time, **CARRIE DENNY** had not yet planned her own wedding, she's been in the biz for years as editor of *Philadelphia* magazine's bridal publication, *Philadelphia Wedding*. She has fielded questions from brides about whether they can "forget" to invite their super-pretty best friend because they think she might show them up on the big day (no); whether it's OK for a bride to blow as much of her budget on a personal trainer as she did on the Dress, just to make sure she looked *that good* in it (yes); and whether it's really that bad if a bride-to-be changes her entire registry when her groom's not looking (maybe). She's spent years as a walking, breathing wedding encyclopedia for her friends, on-call during their engagements like an OB during the ninth month. And yes, when her boyfriend finally cracks, she will be the calmest, coolest, most logical, rational, and non-Bridezilla bride to ever plan a wedding. She lives in Center City, Philadelphia.

About the Illustrators

PAUL KEPPLE and **SCOTTY REIFSNYDER** are better known as the Philadelphia-based studio **HEADCASE DESIGN**. Their work has been featured in many design and illustration publications, such as *AIGA 365* and *50 Books/50 Covers*, *American Illustration*, *Communication Arts*, and *Print*. Paul worked at Running Press Book Publishers for several years before opening Headcase in 1998. Paul graduated from the Tyler School of Art, where he now teaches. Scotty is a graduate of Kutztown University and received his M.F.A. from Tyler School of Art, where he had Paul as an instructor.